W9-BWA-294

HOW
HARD
CAN IT
BE?

HOW HARD CAN IT BE?

ToolGirl's Favorite Repairs and Projects

MAG RUFFMAN

BEYOND
WORDS
Publishing
I N C

To Mum, who always has fun, no matter how hard it can be

Beyond Words Publishing, Inc.
20827 NW Cornell Road, Suite 500
Hillsboro, Oregon 97124-9808
503-531-8700

The photographs on pages xii, xiv, 50, 90, 124, 170, 172, 192 © Korby Banner. All other photographs © Daniel Hunter. The illustrated figures © Bryce Hallett.
All images reprinted by permission of the owners.

Cover photograph: Korby Banner
Interior Design: Cindy Reichle
Proofreaders: Marvin Moore and Jade Chan
Composition: William H. Brunson Typography Services

Printed in the United States of America

Library of Congress Cataloging-in-Publication Data

Ruffman, Mag.
    How hard can it be? : Toolgirl's favorite repairs and projects / Mag Ruffman ;
foreword by Steve Smith ("Red Green").
        p. cm.
    1. Dwellings — Maintenance and repair — Amateurs' manuals.   I. Title.

    TH4817.3.R84   2005
    643'.7— dc22

                                                2005018450

The corporate mission of Beyond Words Publishing, Inc:
  Inspire to Integrity

Contents

Chapter 2 | Outdoor Maintenance   51

Chapter 3 | Upgrades   91

Chapter 5 | Tools and Equipment   171

Foreword

To put Mag Ruffman into perspective, you have to first of all acknowledge how difficult it is to surprise the same people continually over a long period of time. Mag does it with ease. I've known her for almost twenty years, and I still have no idea what she's going to do next. But whatever it is, it will be innovative and interesting and entertaining. My first contact with Mag was when my wife and I were auditioning people for a comedy series called *The Comedy Mill*. She came in to the audition not particularly prepared, but we soon realized we weren't either. She lit up the room. And it was a pretty dark room. Some people have talent. Some people have personality. Mag has both. (Some have neither, but that's what politics is for.) The truth is, Mag has done a lot of things and has had success in all of them. From musical theater to television comedy to film drama to animation to painting to needlework and, of course, to plumbing. Her résumé is twice the size of this book. And above all, she is a great laugher. Whenever she comes to a taping of my show, I can pick out her laughter in any crowd — and not always because she's the only one laughing. That's because Mag is a great friend. She's very easy to talk to. She has a way of listening and supporting whatever it is you're up to, while applying a little gentle nudging through asking questions that you're the only one in the world who can answer. She brings that same attitude to the world of repairs and renovations, convincing us all that we can celebrate rotted floors and leaky basements because they give us an opportunity to empower ourselves in a world that otherwise ignores us. And you're going to realize in this book that Mag is one of those people who can use funny words and still know what she's talking about. Mag can make anything unboring. If I'd known her earlier in high school, I probably would have passed chemistry. Mag has a lot of that too. So I suggest you treat this book as a friend. Read it now for the fun of it and then look after it, and one day when you need it, it will be there for you. That's what Mag does best. When one of my sons was seven or eight years old, we were talking about Mag, whom he'd always liked, and it led to discussing the optimistic approach to life. I asked him, "Is the glass half full or half empty?" He thought for a minute and then answered, "It depends whether you're filling it or emptying it." Mag Ruffman is filling it.

— Steve Smith, *The Red Green Show*

A Note from Mag

I started my career in musical theater, and if I'd stayed with it, these pages would be the script and score of a lively musical about home repair, instead of a book. My musical, entitled *Vent*, would be an all-singing exploration of deep emotions about grout, mold, and furnace filters. Wouldn't you pay eighty bucks to see that?

I figure that by writing a book I'm offering the world a less-expensive and quieter form of entertainment. And I'm not stopping there. As a special bonus, I'm including many in-focus photographs, which offer slightly higher visual accuracy than the rear balcony of most theaters.

By now you might be starting to feel pretty good about this book. But wait, I can make you feel even better. Here's my promise: Even if you've never held a screwdriver, you can successfully complete all the projects and repairs in this book.

The reason I know you can do this stuff is because every chapter has received the Stamp of Improbable Achievement, meaning that someone with extremely limited prospects has already accomplished each task. No telling who that person might be, although her initials are MR, which is two-thirds of Mrs., which means I'm more than slightly married, for those who've been asking.

Consider this: I don't have the physical coordination to make it through a single day without spilling something (coffee, brake fluid, paint stripper) or staining something (furniture, body parts, reputation).

If I can do something badly, you can do it better. I'll applaud your success. Just notify me as soon as you've done something admirable and I'll send you a substandard recording of myself clapping (and possibly singing about ducts and toilet tanks).

But don't send photos of your wonderful project, especially if it came out better than mine, which it will. There's only so much I can take, and most of that is when nobody's looking.

If you're still with me, I'm glad you're willing to join my special club of people who like to try things that build character and sometimes ruin clothing. Be brazen. Be strong. ToolGirls and ToolGuys are the world's secret weapon against negligence and apathy. Together we march against dry rot, gutter gunk, and mildew. We're on fire.

1 INDOOR MAINTENANCE

Some people would call the repairs in this chapter "minor," but that's a scary word. "Minor" doesn't take your personality into account. A repair may be minor for some people, but for others (and I'm usually in the "others" group), it requires reserves of skill and concentration way past what's stashed in our personality wallet. So you can end up in a sort of ego debt. You might not be up to doing what you're trying to do, but the word "minor" keeps reverberating in your ears like a bad 1970s hit. You keep going because your ego says, "It's minor, nimrod." (Notice how the word "nimrod" has the same letters as the word "minor," with the addition of a *d*. That's no accident. D-minor is the key composers use for all repair-themed music.)

Self-Motivation
The best way to deal with ego debt is to give yourself a little pep talk. Here's what I've learned about self-motivation: Never use the first person in your pep talk. Saying "I can do it" is completely ineffectual. Why? Because you don't believe yourself.

Never use the second person either. Because saying "Come on, you can do it" reminds you of every time you've said that to someone who was screwing up badly. So what kind of a message are you sending yourself? An insincere one that's not helpful.

No, if you need a pep talk, use the third person. Example: "She yanked on the toilet, her tight loins straining against the fabric of her jeans." See? The third person adds a sense of observation and distance from the actual repair, while making you appear better toned. If that's not motivating, I don't know what is.

1

Patience

When you're preparing to attempt a repair, always allow yourself triple the time you think it's going to take. Remember, time has a way of moving way faster than the speed of the average repair, so it won't be long before you're so far behind you can see your own rear end.

Reality

The maintenance procedures in this chapter are "minor" in the following ways:

• You don't need very many tools.

• Most of these repairs can be done alone, so no one will ever know how much trouble you got into.

• Instructions include enough technical lingo to enable you to brag about your repair without anyone being able to guess what you actually accomplished.

Grout, Damn Spot!

The importance of sealing grout lines

We've just moved and things are not going well. The basement has an indeterminate funk that has settled in my sinuses, the shower faucet leaks, and there are rodents partying in the attic at 4 AM. I've got ants in places I didn't think you could have ants, and they're producing vast piles of sawdust. Also, it rained the day we moved in, so the piano got wet and now all the white keys have delaminated. This means that I have to play my favorite polkas using only the black keys.

These are the kinds of household setbacks that would torment a great mind. Consequently, I don't suffer. In fact, these problems are a relief. After all, a girl's worst enemy is free time because when the mind wanders, the hands are never far behind. So it's good to be busy. For example, I often keep busy by creating outlines for a dramatic series on housekeeping.

As Sophia Loren said, "Mistakes are part of the dues one pays for a full life." When you've made so many mistakes that you've paid your dues for the next century, you know you have a full life. To me, this is a charitable opportunity. When people complain that their lives are empty, I'm happy to donate some of my mistakes.

Diary of a Bad Homeowner, Episode One
She wakes up facedown beside a pool of spit. Oh wait, it's not spit. It's hydrochloric acid. Well, same thing, really. She rolls away from the caustic puddle, vaguely surprised to find herself napping on the kitchen floor. Then she remembers why she's there. She turns her head and dully surveys the arsenal of household chemicals with which she has tried, and failed, to achieve results. She has the darkest, grimiest grout lines in the country, and so far, no existing substance has lightened the grout to even a rich mocha, let alone white.

She rolls onto her back, the chill of the tile floor penetrating her thin shirt. "How can a highly evolved human be

A day in the life of a bad homeowner.

defeated by simple grime?" she moans, fearing she has the IQ of mildew. (Although, actually, mildew is quite smart. And devious. Anyone with a shower stall knows that. But back to our story.)

She reviews her strategies, struggling to understand. She has scoured her grout lines with trisodium phosphate, Comet, hydrogen peroxide, ammonia, chlorine bleach, tile stripper, lemon juice, vinegar, and baking soda. She has hooked up her Dremel rotary tool and tried various attachments to abrade the grime; the stone-grinding cone sort of worked but kept skidding out of the grout lines, etching exotic patterns on the tile surface. Finally she uses a commercial floor-stripping preparation hopped up with hydrochloric acid, but it too was utterly unhelpful.

She stares at the ceiling, imagining the house years before she'd bought it. Once upon a time, the kitchen floor had been new—*that* would have been the time to apply sealant on the grout lines. But no. Those naked grout lines went untreated until they absorbed every spill and splatter that came their way.

She feels a flicker of pity for the once-resplendent grout, now bonded permanently with the color of neglect. She sighs. Her mood hangs over the room like fumes from a derailed train that had been carrying chemicals through a low-lying area but now sprawls on its side, oozing noxious gases like a rhino in a zoo after a big meal of dank swamp vegetation. *Moral:* If people would just use grout sealant, nobody would ever have the day this woman is having. And cut to cheery detergent commercial.

Like it? Please write the networks.

Seriously, apply grout sealant after you've installed tile, or after stripping a grouted floor. With new tile you'll need to wait a week for the fresh grout to cure fully. Then seal by painting the grout lines with a couple of coats of sealant. It's quick. It's easy. It is *so* worth doing. If you don't believe me, come over to my place and help me with my grimy grout. Bring a blowtorch. Or napalm. Thanks for listening.

SAFETY ALERT!

- Don't ever combine household chemicals, especially chlorine bleach and ammonia. When mixed together they become toxic, acrid, and highly caustic to your lungs.
- Use chemical-resistant nitrile gloves when handling chemicals.
- Wear safety glasses to protect your peepers.
- Observe the caution data on the labels, especially if there's a picture of an explosion.

Filter Tips

Changing your furnace filter

The great James Thurber wrote, "It is better to know some of the questions than all the answers." But when you're trying to locate your furnace filter, you need answers. So if James Thurber was your next-door neighbor, you probably wouldn't want his help with filter mainte-nance. But if he comes over anyway, just give him two bucks and say, "It is better to have some of the money for a six-pack than to have to buy all the beer."

Do you ever wonder what household dust is actually made of? Well, I found out. A lot of it is dead skin. When you scratch, towel off, file your nails, dress or undress, you are discarding bits of dead epidermis, which become household dust. So, in fact, "dusting" the furniture is really "de-skinning." There are other treats mixed in with the dead skin, like pollen, plant and mold spores, pet dander, lint, bacteria, and dust-mite poop.

To make matters worse, most North Americans spend 90 percent of their time indoors. And with all the modern emphasis on efficiency, some homes are so airtight that air-borne particles get trapped indoors and can't escape. This means that the air inside many homes is two to five times more polluted than outdoor air!

Your furnace filter can help your family avoid allergies, asthma, sinus infections, the flu, and bronchitis by lowering the particle count in your home. If your current furnace filter is inefficient, old, or dirty, the air you're breathing is probably thick with particles. A failing filter means the job of cleaning the air falls to your hardworking nose and sinuses, which is probably why our culture is facing a wave of chronic respira-tory diseases, and why Americans spend more than $37 billion a year on costs linked to respiratory problems, according to the American Lung Association (November 2004). By comparison, furnace filters are cheap.

You will find the filter aisle rife with variety. Choosing the right filter is easier than it looks, because many of them are so lame you won't want them. This is what's available:

There's a dizzying array of filters to choose from.

Disposable panel filters, low-priced and virtually useless, shield the blower and coils of your furnace. These babies don't trap smaller airborne contaminants that mess with your health. They're made of cloth, fiberglass, open-cell foam, or synthetic fibers. They're so porous you can see through them. They remove 10 percent or less of the particles from your air (and only the really big ones). They're often sold in three-packs, which camouflages their flimsy composition.

Washable/reusable filters seem like a good idea, but it's hard to get them truly clean even with the garden hose set on Obliterate. Many washable filters are ineffective at capturing small particles and allergens (e.g., smoke), according to research supported by the American Lung Association. If you do decide to use this kind, buy one that is electrostatic and be ruthless in your cleaning procedures.

TIPS

- Make sure your furnace is compatible with the brand of filter you choose. If in doubt, check with the furnace manufacturer.
- A pair of pantyhose does not make an efficient dust filter for your dryer. The last time I bought a second-hand dryer, it came with a pair of support hose tied onto the exhaust. Each leg was swollen with dryer lint. The person who sold me the dryer explained that the pantyhose acts as both lint collector and humidifier, since the moist air from the dryer fills the house after escaping the pantyhose. I said, "So that explains your persistent cough." Please ensure your dryer is properly vented. End of lecture.
- For more information, visit www.lungusa.org.

Pleated filters are just flat filters with pleats, which increase the surface area so more particles are collected. However, these filters can get clogged up with particles, making it harder for air to pass through, so your fan works harder and your furnace runs longer. Therefore you must change these filters frequently to ensure proper airflow. **High-efficiency pleated filters** are made of electrostatically charged fibers designed to attract tiny particles that other filters don't catch, including smoke. High-efficiency filters, like the Filtrete from 3M, capture up to thirty times more allergens than standard fiberglass filters. The Filtrete is recommended by the American Lung Association. Since really small particles are the worst culprits, making up 99 percent of contaminants in indoor air, these filters are a great idea. Replace them every three months. They cost about $25 and are well worth it. You'll breathe better, and you won't have to dust as often.

Getting Started

Before changing your filter, turn off the power to the furnace fan by using the switch on the furnace, or by turning your home's thermostat off. Locate the filter. This can be straightforward or irritating, depending on your furnace model and your level of alertness. *Hint:* Your filter is located in the return grill, in the main return near the furnace, or inside the furnace near the blower. It could also be hidden behind a door or panel that lifts or swings open. The door or panel will be indistinguishable from the rest of the ductwork, and it won't open without a fight. If you can't find the filter, blame your parents for their choices that somehow led to you living in a cold climate where you have to know stuff about furnaces. Then consult the furnace manual. If all else fails, call a heating contractor and watch him or her change the filter.

For future reference, paint huge arrows all over the furnace indicating the location of the filter.

Out with the Old and In with the New
Grasp the edge of the filter and slide it out of its channel. Before installing, look for an arrow on the edge of your new filter. This arrow indicates the required direction of airflow. Position the filter so the arrow points toward the blower motor and related machinery. Putting the filter in backwards decreases its efficiency, so get it right.

Timing Is Everything
Most households should replace filters every three months. However, if you've been doing dusty renovations, burning candles, or smoking inside the house, you'll need to change your filter more often. If anyone in your family suffers from asthma, allergies, or breathing problems, try changing your filter monthly to keep the indoor air as clean as possible. As an additional precaution, run your furnace fan continuously throughout the year. The filter can only trap contaminants if the blower is running.

Wet It Be

Handling condensation problems in basements

There's an old saying that nothing is really work unless you'd rather be doing something else, so whenever I feel like I'd rather be doing something else, I do it. That way when I'm ninety-five I'll be able to say, "I've never worked a day in my life" and everyone at the nursing home will think I'm rich.

It was a dank and steamy night. The house smelled acrid, and this time it wasn't my cooking. My cooking doesn't smell like mildewy running shoes, unless I fry cabbage, and I don't fry cabbage. So no, it wasn't my cooking. But the air smelled bad. Like a wet dog. Only I don't have a dog. The process of elimination was wearing me out. But I had to know where the odor was coming from.

I found myself in the basement. Not philosophically but literally. The smell was worse there. I opened the door to the laundry room. The stink hit me like a fat man in a bad suit. When I came to, I needed more than a stiff drink. I needed a dehumidifier.

The fact is, we had just moved in a week ago. It wasn't hot and humid when we bought the place, so it had smelled fine. But now the laundry room reeked like a barn full of cats with slack personal hygiene. It was my job to eliminate the stench.

I looked no further than the rotting carpet under the plumbing lines. Stained with old lime, that carpet had a look I hadn't seen since the 1970s, and I didn't like the 1970s. I tugged on a corner of the carpet. Some bonehead had glued it to the subfloor. My evening was just getting better and better because now I could use my brand-new carpet knife. I made short work of ripping the carpet into strips and pulling it up. The plywood underneath was as damp and spongy as a damp sponge. It was so mushy I could've written my name in it. But I wasn't in the mood for calligraphy.

I looked around. Water was collecting in that basement like teenagers in a convenience store parking lot. The concrete

A hygrometer measures temperature and moisture level.

Mildew sucks! Don't let this happen to you.

walls and cold-water pipes were covered in condensation, which was dripping steadily onto the floor. It was bad. I needed to know how bad. I whipped out my pocket hygrometer. It registered 68 percent relative humidity. The only time I've seen readings that high was in the summer of 1989 in the back of a van. This basement was in trouble.

Prolonged dampness is a Sunday picnic for mildew, mold, and rot. In hot, humid weather, moisture condenses on the coldest surface available. It happens in basements, and it happens on beer bottles. But just slide one of those classy foam jackets onto a beer bottle and, bingo, no more condensation. That gave me an idea.

I set up a fan to blow air across the soggy plywood. The light breeze would drive off some of the moisture, but it wouldn't be nearly enough, not with 68 percent relative humidity.

SAFETY ALERT!

• Can I be your mother, just for a moment? "Quit that or you'll put your eye out!" Wear safety glasses when using a utility knife or carpet blade. The blades can break and go flying.

• B-I-N primer is alcohol-based. You'll get woozy if you breathe the fumes. Wear a respirator mask and make sure the work area is well ventilated.

I needed to think. I slipped out into the night and got into my truck. The engine kicked in like the startled rasp of an adolescent boy with adenoid trouble. I started to drive.

Sure, I could insulate the pipes with those preformed foam sleeves they sell at the hardware store. But did I have to insulate every square inch of the cold walls and air-conditioning ducts too? Or was there some other way to stop moisture from condensing on the cold surfaces? What about the sodden subfloor? Should I rip it out and replace it, or wait until it dried to see if it still stunk? And how was I going to get the subfloor dry in 68 percent humidity?

By the time I pulled into the hardware store parking lot, I was calm. I picked up a dehumidifier to reduce the basement's humidity. I got three lengths of foam sleeving for the plumbing pipes, and one gallon of Zinsser B-I-N stain-blocking primer to seal the plywood subfloor once it dried. The primer would lock any stink in and protect the plywood from growing more mildew. Then, as an afterthought, I went for an additional gallon of mildew-resistant porch and floor paint, because once mildew invades, it lurks like an evil warlord in a historical romance novel.

I drove home and wrapped the pipes with the self-sealing foam sleeves. Easier than putting doll clothes on a cat. Next I plugged in the dehumidifier. It was humming contentedly when I closed the door to the laundry room and went to bed my favorite way: smiling. The next morning that dehumidifier had sucked a gallon of water out of the air and it was still pulling. I was a happy woman, but there was one thing that could make me even happier. I connected a garden hose to the dehumidifier and ran it to the basement drain. Now I'll never have to check the dehumidifier reservoir again.

Just as I was thinking it doesn't get much better than this, it did. I whipped out my hygrometer again. Down to 36 percent. My heart beat a little faster. The plywood was dry now, so I vacuumed, cracked open the B-I-N primer, and sealed the whole floor. No more residual moldy smell. No more condensation, anywhere.

Maybe someday humans will grow nose hairs fine enough to strain mildew spores out of the atmosphere. But until then, mildew is just botany gone horribly wrong. Let's fight this thing in the basements and in the bathrooms, until one day, old people will say, "Remember that time we had that mildew problem?" And none of the youngsters will know what they're talking about.

Ants Go Marching

Carpenter ants

Remember summer pajama parties when you were eleven and all the kids used to pile into a tent and tell ghost stories and scare the pants off each other? And remember how there was always one kid hiding at the bottom of her sleeping bag with a really loud transistor radio so she couldn't hear the scary story? Then at the end of the story when everyone screamed, she screamed the loudest and then barfed? That was me. I was overly sensitive.

So when I found out that carpenter ants were living inside my walls and that if I didn't stop them from chewing the framing to bits I would soon be sleeping in a tent again, I knew I needed a strategy. I went to my room, plunged my head under my pillow, and tuned my shortwave radio to Helsinki, where, as far as I could make out, things were going perfectly well.

Sometimes I like to ask myself probing questions, like where did the years go, and why is my left arm numb? If my repairs have gone well, I celebrate with my lucky beverage: beer. If things have not gone well, I drink something more humbling. Prune juice is good.

After several minutes of upbeat Finnish banter, I felt energized and even cocky. I went back downstairs and looked at the pile of sawdust beside the front door. I watched ants emerge from a tiny hole at the base of the doorjamb, drop tiny chunks of my framing onto the porch floor, and disappear back into the wall.

There is one reason why carpenter ants move into houses: moisture. Carpenter ants don't like chewing tough, dry wood; it cracks their molars. They like their wood wet or even rotten — the better to sculpt lovely smooth chambers in which to raise ant babies.

How bad can it be? One exterminator reported treating a place in cottage country for a colony of 150,000 ants, all chewing like baseball players during a bad inning. He could hear those ants with the naked ear: an insistent, scrabbling sound coming from inside the walls under large (leaky) picture windows. Creepy? I'm in my sleeping bag just writing about it.

Pulling soil away from the house to eliminate wood-to-ground contact.

How to Know If You've Got 'Em

Carpenter ants come in many castes, sizes, and colors, so it's easier to identify them by their location and behavior rather than appearance. Here are their favorite locations:

- Inside the walls next to poorly caulked doors, windows, bathtubs, showers, and sinks, or improperly grouted shower pans
- Inside walls or under floors near steady or intermittent plumbing leaks
- In attics near plugged gutters
- In firewood (mostly softwood — e.g., pine or poplar) stored outdoors, near the bottom of the pile where it stays damp
- Anywhere around the outside of your home where soil is in contact with wood framing or siding

Your primary tip-off is *frass* — a pile of excavated wood particles mixed with dead insect body parts and ant poop. Active ants in the vicinity of a frass pile means you have an infestation.

A pile of sawdust called *frass* indicates an active infestation.

What You Can Try

Follow the ants to discover the whereabouts of the nest(s). They're more active at night, so stake out frass piles with snack food and a flashlight. Once you find their main entry points, you can call an exterminator or try solving the problem yourself.

If you go the DIY (do-it-yourself) route, don a dust mask and use a plastic ketchup dispenser to blow acid powder (not crystals!) into the holes, cracks, and crevices around the nest. Boric acid powder is somewhat slower acting (three to ten days) than synthetic pesticides, but it's extremely long-lasting. Boric acid was used on the wood in Stradivarius's violins, and that's why those instruments are still around today.

What Exterminators Use

Exterminators are fast and efficient and guarantee their work. They'll apply a three-inch band of perimeter spray outside, along the base of your foundation, and inside at floor level in the affected area. In addition, they'll use a powder that is 99 percent talc, puffing it into the nest in the same way I described the application of boric acid powder.

The perimeter spray Permethrin is a popular synthetic that mimics the African chrysanthemum resins found in natural pyrethrin. Permethrin is much more stable than natural "chrysanthemum dust" and is effective for thirty days, while natural pyrethrins start breaking down within hours.

On the downside, recent government and independent studies show that some synthetic pyrethroids can cause reproductive problems, dermal and respiratory allergies, neurotoxicity, kidney and liver damage, disruption of the endocrine system, and enhanced risk of breast cancer. So if your exterminator says it's "as safe as chrysanthemum flowers" but he or she is using a synthetic such as Permethrin, your exterminator doesn't have all the facts.

No, Permethrin isn't harmful once the airborne spray has settled, unless you lick it. Perhaps you can live with that. Visit www.beyondpesticides.org for more information. And take your transistor radio.

Talking to Exterminators

If you go with an exterminator, request the least toxic application it has. Some companies will give you many reasons not to worry about the health or environmental risks of pesticides and may convince you that conventional pesticides are more effective than less toxic alternatives. Don't give in. In virtually all cases of pest management, there are excellent preventative measures not associated with the high risk of pesticide poisoning. Be a hero to your home, and don't tempt noble carpenter ants away from the outdoors, where they do their job of helping to decompose fallen trees so willingly and so well.

Dishwasher Cheese

The other white meat

William Blake said, "Exuberance is beauty." It would've been fun to date William Blake instead of that one boyfriend I had who kept saying, "You're beautiful when you're quiet." Being quiet is hard. So it can take a long time to find the right guy.

People often struggle with vocabulary related to construction, hardware, and appliances. They simply lack the technical lingo. Here is a helpful glossary of terms that may be useful to the modern homeowner:

Dishwasher cheese: A compressed, feltlike layer of food that has fused to your dishwasher strainer and gaskets if you never rinse your dishes before placing them in the unit. Dishwasher cheese causes film and grime on dishes, smells acrid, has the consistency of fried feta, and may even be combustible. Opa!

"What the —": The first two words out of a homeowner's mouth upon encountering dishwasher cheese.

"Right, I see...": The first three words out of a customer service rep's mouth when you call a manufacturer's toll-free number to describe the problem you're having with an appliance. Once you've been disarmed by the rep's display of concurrence, you're willing to do anything she suggests, including pulling your dishwasher out from under the counter so you can read the serial number on the back of it, which you won't be able to read because it's obscured by corrosion, a cousin of dishwasher cheese. Meanwhile the customer service rep waits for you with barely a trace of annoyance as you scrape your way down to the serial number, which, when found, triggers the rep to announce with sudden coldness that your dishwasher was built in the 1960s and they no longer make parts for that model.

She: The pronoun used by many independent dishwasher repairmen to identify an appliance that's malfunctioning,

Ugh! A cheesy undertaking.

as in, "'Way she's sounding, she's probably got a cheese buildup."

Trap: The curiously named U-shaped under-sink pipe through which your dishwasher usually drains. The trap contains standing water to block sewer gases from backing up and entering your home. Traps usually haven't been cleaned out since the 1960s, so the slime they harbor may be sentient. Place your slime under a microscope and see if it responds to basic commands. If it does, send prize-winning footage to *America's Most Amazing Botany Videos*.

Effluvium, effluvia, effluxion: A family of terms related to noxious trap fumes, or any deadly gas, as in, "After the chili, I effluxed a pound of carbon emissions."

Reef: An effort of extreme force, as in, "I really had to reef on those nuts."

Fittings: An ironic term describing plumbing parts that don't fit together, no matter how hard you reef on them.

Cheese Triage

If you encounter the heartbreak of dishwasher cheese, try the following:

1. Run your finger along the hard-to-see edges of gaskets and feel for encrustation. When you detect the gritty mucilaginous crud, scream, "What the — !"
2. Pour a gallon of vinegar into the bottom of the dishwasher and set the unit on rinse.
3. Let the dishwasher cool and, if possible, remove the strainer. (The strainer is under the lower spray arm.)
4. Use a scrub brush dipped in vinegar to scour the gasket and strainer surfaces.
5. Replace the strainer.
6. Run the unit with vinegar once again.
7. Rinse your dishes from now on.

If you have any helpful terms to submit to the *ToolGirl Dictionary of Home Repair Slang*, please feel free to send them to toolgirl@anythingicando.com.

Washer, I Hardly Know Her!

Changing a defunct washer

R emember the last time you wrote down your life goals? Did you forget to add "Learn to change a washer" to that list? I can help.

First, consider the following:
• The polar ice caps contain 70 percent of the world's supply of fresh water.
• Russia's Lake Baikal contains 20 percent of the world's supply of freshwater.
• That leaves only 10 percent for the six billion of us who don't live in Antarctica or own a cottage on Lake Baikal.

Also consider:
• A faucet leaking a tiny stream of water (1/16-inch diameter) wastes 74,000 gallons of drinking water in three months (the average procrastination period of homeowners and landlords).
• A faucet leaking a wider stream of water (1/4-inch diameter) wastes 1,181,500 gallons in three months.

If you learn how to fix a leaky faucet, you actually help preserve the global population's available drinking water supply. Therefore, it follows that you can revise your life goals and immediately check off "Initiate environmental solutions for the whole planet."

Congratulations on this milestone. But you'll be pleased to know there are even more benefits to knowing how to change a washer:
1. More sleep, thanks to quiet, non-drippy faucets
2. More cash, thanks to lower water bills

S ometimes I like to attempt repairs that I have no idea how to do. I take my inspiration from a guy named Doug Larson, who once said, "Some of the world's greatest feats were accomplished by people not smart enough to know they were impossible." Apparently a lifetime of ignorance can really pay off. I'm willing to go for it.

TIPS

• Use an open end or box end wrench on the brass packing nut. These are precision tools that won't mar the delicate brass. Avoid adjustable crescent wrenches. They don't stay tight on the packing nut and you'll end up rounding off the nut's edges and then you'll be totally, horribly screwed and that's being conservative.

• If your washer is torn or scratched up, you may have a worn valve seat that's chewing up the washer and causing the leaky faucet. The valve seat is located in the very bottom of the valve. Go ahead, check. You can see it sitting down there, staring defiantly up at you like a Cyclops with a hexagonal (or sometimes square) eye. You can replace most valve seats using a seat wrench, an inexpensive L-shaped tool (continued on p. 23)

3. More dinners, cooked for you by people whose leaky faucets you fixed

4. More confidence in bars

Changing a washer takes about five minutes if everything goes well. It won't go well, but keep repeating, "Oh yeah, baby, bring it on" as things get worse. This aggressive tactic will earn the respect of the plumbing gods.

Steps

1. Start by shutting off the water supply to the leaky faucet. If there isn't an individual valve (look under the sink) supplying the tap in question, find the main water supply valve and shut off the water to the entire dwelling. If you're not sure which way to turn the valve handle, remember the plumbing anthem, "Righty tighty, lefty loosey." (i.e., Turning the handle all the way to the *right* closes the valve *tight*, so no water flows. Turning the handle all the way to the *left loosens* the valve and opens the flow of water.) You could also just wait until someone is having a shower, and then you'll get instant audible feedback confirming that the water is now off.

2. Turn the leaky tap(s) to the On position to drain the lines. Plug the sink to preclude coarse language caused by dropping parts down the drain.

3. Study your tap handle. Most handles have a decorative cap that hides the working parts. You have to figure out how to remove this cover, button, or tab. Some of them are totally baffling, but they all come off. Usually a flathead screwdriver or knife blade easily lifts the decorative cap.

4. After prying off the cap, you should see a screw, usually a Phillips (the kind with an X stamped in the head). Remove it with a screwdriver that fits really snugly. Push down hard enough as you turn the screw that you actually grunt. This ensures that the screwdriver won't slip and strip the screw head.

Step 3: Removing the decorative cap.

Step 4: Removing the retaining screw.

TIPS

(continued from p. 22) with one hexagonal end and one square end. All you have to do is unscrew the valve seat, buy an identical one, and replace it. There is, however, one kind of valve that doesn't allow you to replace the valve seat, and that valve is usually located in the position where the main water supply comes into your house. In that case, you'll have to grind the valve seat smooth with a seat-grinding tool, since you can't simply replace the valve seat. Is this more than you ever wanted to know about plumbing?

5. Pull the tap handle up and off. Take a moment to marvel at how well this is going.

6. You should now see the top of the "stem" and the hexagonal outline of the brass packing nut. To loosen the nut, use a tight-fitting mechanic's wrench that won't strip the soft brass. If you must use tongue-and-groove pliers, cover the "teeth" with duct tape so they don't tear up the brass.

Step 6: Loosening the packing nut.

7. (a) Pull the whole stem assembly up and out. At the bottom of the stem is a small brass screw that holds a washer (usually black rubber) in position. Eureka! If it's compressed or has grooves in it, replacing it will probably cure your faucet's leak.

(b) If your *handle* has been leaking, you have a different problem. Unscrew the packing nut from the stem. (The stem is slippery, so pop the handle back onto the stem and you'll get a better grip.) Once you have the packing nut off, you'll

see a rubber O-ring riding in a groove on the stem.
If it's torn or squished, you need to replace it.

8. There are about 3,498 tap configurations in the world.
Washers and O-rings range wildly in size, shape, and thickness. So take the *entire stem* with you to the hardware store
and exactly match the parts you need to replace, or buy a
whole new identical stem if that's the mood you're in.

9. (a) When you get home, remove the old, gnarly washer by
undoing the screw at the bottom of the stem. Set the plump,
frisky new washer in position. Retighten the screw.

Step 9(a): Removing the screw that holds the rubber washer in place.

(b) If necessary, remove the old O-ring and install a new
one. If you have some plumber's silicone grease, coat the
O-ring with it before putting it back in place. Screw
the packing nut back onto the stem and drop it into position. Hand-tighten the packing nut, then tighten it a further
half-turn using your wrench.

10. Replace the handle and reinstall the screw and decorative tab. Turn the tap to the Off position.

11. Go back to the water supply and open the valve by turning it "lefty loosey." Check to make sure the leak is gone.

That's it. Put your tools away and enjoy a tall, cool glass of the drinking water you just rescued, you radiant conservationist, you.

Caulk Sure

Maintaining your caulk

> Bertrand Russell said, "The trouble with the world is that the stupid are cocksure and the intelligent are full of doubt." I've discovered the happy medium of assuming that all my doubts are stupid, while acting smarter than I look.

Sometimes I look at all the new subdivisions going up and marvel at the amount of caulk that goes into them. If you added it all up, you'd have more caulk than you'd know what to do with. But you can never have too much caulk, because even a high-end caulk shrinks after it's been left alone for a while.

Shrunken caulk syndrome is every homeowner's nightmare. Here are the signs: There are gaps between the baseboard and the walls, spaces around the window trim, crevices over the kitchen backsplash, and dark ditches around the tub. The caulk is no longer doing its job. Don't take it personally; it happens to everyone at some point.

Beefing up deteriorated caulk results in a much cleaner appearance in all the rooms of your home. If you're living in a new subdivision, you'll know what I'm talking about. The place looked great when you moved in, but after the first year, those gaps start to distract the eye and make the interior feel worn.

The worst part is that in some new homes, the caulk around windows and doors needs to be repaired right away or the house leaks warm air in winter. Your heating bills will be higher because poorly caulked windows and doors lose as much heat as leaving a small window wide open all winter. Don't let this happen to you. Grab your caulk and get on with it.

For repairs to interior gaps between painted surfaces, you'll need paintable latex caulk. This is the "everyman" of caulks. It is easy to work with, odor-free, and cleans up nicely with water. It sticks to drywall, wood, plaster, and masonry. Different brands are guaranteed for durability from five to thirty-five years. Buy the best. If you're recaulking in a kitchen or bathroom, get the paintable latex caulk with silicone in it; it's mildew-resistant for damp rooms. (However, don't recaulk the *tub* with this stuff. You need something special for that.)

It's best to apply the caulk with the tub full of water.

TIPS

• Avoid the awkwardness of a caulking gun and use Loctite Press and Seal sealant—a convenient tube with a built-in trigger that delivers a completely dripless, delicate bead of high-quality caulk.

• If you're all thumbs, use the Caulk-Rite tool, a small, rounded spatula that gives your bead a perfect, clean finish.

• Removing older caulks can be trouble. Try DAP Caulk-Be-Gone Caulk Remover. It's specially formulated to soften caulk for easy removal.

• There are so many caulks to choose from. The range can be bewildering, but you really only need three things in a caulk: endurance, endurance, endurance.

Caulk on the Wild Side

Replacing old caulk in the bathroom is not for the squeamish. But if the seal has failed, water will end up seeping down the walls behind the tub and oozing onto the subfloor. The subfloor gradually rots, and eventually the bathtub sinks through the floor. I actually know a guy who fell through his bathroom floor and landed on the kitchen counter on the first floor. So when the old caulk ain't what it used to be, replace it.

Make the job fun. Scrape away the old, foul mildewy stuff with a paint scraper or sharp knife. This may take a while. Think pleasant thoughts, since this is a disgusting activity. This isn't the fun part yet. Once you have the old caulk out, clean the joint with rubbing alcohol and a scrubby sponge to remove soap scum; otherwise the new caulk won't stick. Let it dry; use a hair dryer to speed things up.

OK, now for the fun part. Get naked. Fill the bathtub (but don't get any water in your freshly clean, dry joint). The weight of the water pulls the metal or fiberglass of your tub into its fully expanded position so that the joint between the tub and the wall is as wide as it will ever be. This means that the new caulk won't get pulled out by tub movement, unless you habitually bathe with six or seven other people, in which case, talk one of *them* into doing the recaulking.

Bad Chair Day

Fixing a wobbly chair one way or another

Chairs get loose over the years, and who can blame them. Torque and friction take their toll. Just ask anyone who's married.

Expecting not to be irritated when you're fixing something is folly. You learn to welcome irritation as part of every project. The more irritated you get, the better the beer tastes when you're done.

Playing doctor with a wobbly chair.

Sonny and Chair

But why wait for a heavyset preteen to flatten a loose-runged dining-room chair in front of judgmental relatives? Actually, that would be funny. Better than it happening to portly older relatives, especially if you owe them money.

TIPS

• Use a cabinet scraper (an inexpensive, rectangular piece of steel with sharp edges) to scrape old adhesive off. It's faster than sanding.

• For removing old adhesive from the inside surface of circular mortises, glue a strip of sandpaper onto a dowel, insert the dowel into your drill, and then ream the hole. Don't overdo it, though, or you'll make the mortise too big for the corresponding rung or spindle.

• If you don't have enough clamps, try using an old plastic jump rope to bind the freshly glued parts together.

There are two ways to fix a wobbly chair: my way or the efficient way. My way means dismantling your rickety chair lovingly, piece by piece, flossing its nooks and crannies, and reassembling it. My way is quite Zen. Unfortunately, Zen is slow, so you may opt for the high-speed alternative of using a miracle product that fixes your chair in no time, with no trouble and no mess.

But I'm torn here, because if you're a person who enjoys the sheer futility of doing things the hard way, I don't want to spoil your fun. Besides, we boneheads have to stick together. So let's cover my way first.

Tools
Hair dryer and/or kettle (optional), vise, rubber mallet, various scrapers, pocket knife, clamps or surgical tubing

Materials
Wet rags, vinegar (optional), sandpaper, carpenter's glue, wood shavings and/or sawdust, toothpicks (optional)

Older furniture is put together with glue made from animal hides. Hide glue crystallizes as it ages, and it's unable to flex when the joint expands and contracts with humidity changes and weight-bearing duties. So the glue ends up failing, and that's when the chair gets shaky.

To fix the unsteady joint, you can remove the hide glue and replace it with modern flexible wood glue, composed of (*Alert:* great conversation starter) long-chain polymers that crosslink to form a strong, supple bond. (Research shows higher dating scores for single people who can use the words "crosslink," "supple," and "bond" in one sentence.)

Getting rid of old crystallized hide glue can be tricky. Even though a joint is miserably unstable, the pieces may not come apart when you reef on them. The good news is that hide glue is water-soluble, so you can soak the joints apart by packing wet rags around them. Once the water seeps into the joint, the glue dissolves and you're on your way. Hopefully. Unless you got everything too wet and the wood swelled and now it's really stuck. In which case, try aiming a hair dryer at the joint for a minute, and see if the heat helps lube things up. You can also boil a kettle underneath the trouble spot and hope the steam loosens it, or try squirting a little vinegar into the joint to dissolve the old hide glue. See how much fun this is? Why cheat yourself by falling back on a simple, easy alternative?

Strip Joints

OK, next, using a rubber mallet (or a hammer covered with a thick cloth), tap the joints apart. It's helpful to clamp one leg of the chair in a vise so you're not chasing it around. Work back and forth from one side to the other so you don't rack the joints, causing them to bind. If you're really having a struggle, a car jack works, and I'm not even kidding.

When you get the chair apart, scrape and sand all the exposed joints, including the mortises (holes). It's really important to get down to bare wood. That's the only way you'll get a good new bond. If you leave any old glue, the new glue will just be glued to the old glue, not to the wood. But the old glue is crummy and it'll just let go of the new glue so the joints will get loose all over again. Talk about a bum deal.

Gap Trap

When you've removed all the old glue, try dry-fitting the joints together. They're likely to be even looser now that all the glue is gone. For small gaps, try Chair Doctor Glue, which is composed of 45 percent solids, so it has great gap-filling properties. You can also try adding your own filler (e.g., sawdust) to regular carpenter's glue. If you have generous gaps to fill, steal a shaving from the potpourri bowl and wrap it

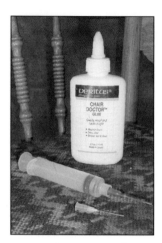

Veritas Chair Doctor Glue.

around the end of the rung, gluing it in place before inser-tion. Or, if you've got a huge gap, you can shove toothpicks into the joint to tighten things up.

Clamp the freshly glued joints in place and leave the chair in peace overnight to give the glue a chance to cure nicely.

Speed versus Zen

Now, if my way doesn't sound like the best Saturday afternoon ever, you can try this simple, efficient, inexpensive alternative:

Treat yourself to Chair Doctor Glue ($10 or under, Lee Valley Tools, www.leevalley.com), which includes an applica-tor syringe and three needles in varying sizes for injecting glue into loose joints. The glue is quite runny, so it pene-trates the narrowest gaps and then wicks into the grain of the wood and swells the wood fibers. As the glue cures, it dries hard inside the cells of the wood, freezing the fibers in that swollen state, and hence, you're left with lovely, permanent, tight joints.

I admit, Chair Doctor Glue registers very high on the Oh, Baby Scale. Whichever way you choose to go with this repair, if you're living with loose, potentially deadly chairs, this could be your most favorite weekend ever.

Strippin' and Screwin' in All the Wrong Places

Repairing stripped screw holes

We've all taken a knob to the forehead by yanking a drawer-pull out by the roots. If this hasn't happened to you, you're probably knob-intolerant and have chosen to hang your socks and underwear on specialized hangers in your closet instead of facing the unpredictability of a knob-inclusive lifestyle.

But if you're a regular person, you've stripped a screw or two in your day. You may have started early in life, swinging happily on a garden gate pretending to be Flying Magnifico at the circus until the hinge-screws failed and your act ended with crying and running into the house, the gate lying prone in the dust.

Remember on *The Carol Burnett Show* when Tim Conway got his pants stuck on the doorknob and he just hung there with his feet dangling and couldn't get off the doorknob even though he tried really hard and Carol and Harvey Corman were incapable of continuing the skit for five full minutes? Well, I've tried that at home. My weight ripped the hinges out of the door. I was hurt in many ways. So after a lifetime of physical emergencies brought on by failing screws, I've built up an arsenal of tips.

Repairing a stripped screw hole is satisfying, with a comparatively low risk of injury. The goal is to plug the hole with something that has the proper density to hold the threads of the original screw (or a new one if you're not trying to maintain an object's authenticity).

When it comes to putting things in holes, people are creative. For example, here is a list of materials that human ingenuity has called upon to help repair stripped-out screw holes in everything from water skis to bassoons. Check off the ones you've tried.

Wooden golf tees
Lead solder
Fishing line
Putty

> If at any point you find you're not happy with your project, it's usually a bad idea to ask anybody else for their opinion. Remember the words of Franklin P. Jones, who said, "Honest criticism is hard to take, particularly from a relative, a friend, an acquaintance, or a stranger."

Potpourri
Chopsticks
Cotton balls soaked in carpenter's glue
Auto-body filler (Bondo)
Steel wool
Softwood matchsticks
Round hardwood toothpicks
Flat softwood toothpicks

My favorite materials for repairing stripped screw holes in wood.

The mind reels, doesn't it? Before trying any of these materials you can also use a longer or fatter screw that will reach sound wood. But where's the irritation in that? If the repair is that easy, do you really want to be involved? No. Because easy repairs can't be bragged about. The difficulty level of a repair is directly proportional to the fun you'll have telling people how you got that scar.

Now, when you're deciding what to plug a hole with, the trick is to match the strength of the existing material. For example, if you've got a stripped screw hole in a pine object, and you fill the hole with a hardwood dowel, you may find that when you drive the screw in, the expanding hardwood acts as a wedge, splitting the surrounding pine.

On the other hand, if you use hole-filling material that's too soft, crumbly, or yielding, the screw will just strip out again and you'll be repeating this repair, only now you'll be annoyed, so things start badly and then get worse in unexpected ways. If you don't believe me, you should see my piano.

Steps

1. Try retightening the loose screw (or drawer pull) in the hole. If that works, great. You're done. If it just spins in place, you need to move on to #2.

2. Remove the loose screw. This can be a pain. Tip the object to get the screw to drop out, or use a magnet or a pair of needle-nose pliers to pull the screw out.

3. Determine, if possible, what kind of wood you're dealing with and what kind of grain you're screwing into. In some cases, the wood will be exceedingly crumbly and difficult to anchor into, so you'll need to fill the hole, *plus* use a longer screw.

4. Choose a filler material based on the hardness of the wood you're dealing with. If you can't tell what kind of wood you've got, use softwood matches, toothpicks, or, my favorite, cotton balls drenched in carpenter's glue.

5. For toothpicks or matchsticks, dip the ends in carpenter's glue and insert enough of them to fill the hole snugly. If you're using gluey cotton balls, stuff as much as you can into the hole (using the tip of a small screwdriver) until the goo is flush with the surface of the surrounding wood.

6. Let it dry. Toothpicks/matchsticks set up in about an hour. Gluey cotton batting takes overnight.

The hole stuffed with my favorite plugging materials.

7. Score the exposed ends of the toothpicks or matchsticks using a utility knife, and then break them off flush with the surface of the surrounding wood. Sand if necessary.

8. Use an awl to make a pilot hole.

9. Insert the screw. If this is very difficult, drill a small pilot hole and try again. Increase the size of the pilot hole as necessary. Don't risk forcing the screw and splitting the wood or stripping the head of the screw, which is a whole other headache.

10. Test your repair by swinging on the object. (Just kidding!)

Door and Peace

Easy tune-up for binding doors

Bathroom time is private time, unless you have a door that won't quite close, in which case bathroom time is ravaged by uncertainty, particularly on days when the cleaners are around.

To determine exactly why your door isn't closing properly, you need sleuthing skills, fortitude, and possibly a helper. Of these three requirements, the helper is the one who can really screw things up. You will be working in extreme proximity to this person, so choose someone who's cheerful and a frequent bather.

Every sticky door has its own reasons for going wacky. Your unique door problem may stem from one or more of the following:

• Hinge issues: Failing screws, bent hinges, sloppy hinge installation.

• House issues: Settling problems or structural framing shrinkage that may have racked the doorjambs.

• Door issues: Door shrinkage, door joints coming apart, latch hardware that needs adjusting.

• Paint issues: Exterior doors that haven't been painted on the top and bottom edges can absorb water and swell badly, making them bind. Alternately, too many coats of paint can make a door too large to fit its opening.

• Humidity issues: Sometimes doors only stick seasonally; the swelling may be occurring in the door or the frame or both.

• Installation issues: Even with some factory pre-hung doors in brand-new houses, there can be binding problems that weren't corrected by the carpenter who installed the doors.

There's an old proverb written by a Scottish person to cheer up other Scottish people: "Be happy while you're living, for you're a long time dead." That proverb makes you realize the importance of being happy, but how can you be, because their logic really bums you out?

TIPS

• Sometimes a door is sitting crookedly in the frame because one of the hinges has been mortised too deeply in the door frame. You can adjust the hinge by loosening the screws, shoving shims (e.g., scraps of wood, folded paper, or toothpicks) under the hinge plate, and then retightening the screws.

A non-closing door is a bane to the privacy-loving bathroom enthusiast.

Sleuth or Consequences

Deciding which problem(s) you have is the sleuthing part. Pore over your door searching for clues. When you look at your door as it sits in the frame, you should see an even 1/8-inch gap around the outside edge of the whole door. If the gap is not consistent, your sleuthing job has begun. Here are some additional tips to help:

• Ninety percent of binding trouble can be traced to the hinges.

• If the door is binding near the top on the latch side, the problem is usually a loose top hinge.

• If the latch isn't lining up and catching, the door may be warped and/or the strike plate may need to be moved.

• If none of the hinges are loose, crooked, or bent but the door is still binding on the threshold or top jamb, then either the door *or* the frame is racked. You'll have to take the door off and trim it to fit the opening.

Bear in mind that there are often several things wrong with a door. You can fix the hinges and then the latch doesn't work. You can plane the edge of the door only to discover that the real problem is with the hinges, and now you're really ticked. Remember, mood control is the highest attainment of home maintenance.

On the Loose

Since loose hinges cause most door problems, it's reassuring to know that the solution is fairly basic. Just shove a wooden shim or thin book under the bottom edge of the door to support its weight. Then remove the loose hinge screw and insert wooden matchsticks and/or toothpicks into the hole with a dab of carpenter's glue. Allow twenty minutes for the glue to dry and then reinstall the screw. Longer screws (three-inch screws usually work well) may also help attach the hinge securely to the stud hiding behind the doorjamb. For more ways to fix loose hinge screws, turn to "Strippin' and Screwin' in All the Wrong Places" on page 32.

turn to "Strippin' and Screwin' in All the Wrong Places" on page 32.

SAFETY ALERT!

• Eye protection!

Case in Point
Let me demonstrate how tricky this door thing can be. One of my bathrooms is situated in a recent addition to my home. The bathroom door is hinged to an exterior wall that runs along the back of the house. That wall is evidently settling, pulling the interior framing with it. So the door frame is getting pulled out of shape, forming a slight parallelogram, which is why the perfectly rectangular door won't close. And since the cleaning lady is coming today, I'm planning to ensure that she doesn't surprise my husband in the shower like she did last week. Not that she complained.

Tools
Pencil, hammer, screwdriver, shims or books, ruler, utility knife (optional), plane or saw.

Hinge at the Thought
Naturally, it's easier to refit the door than to jack up a two-story wall. Close the door as far as it will go and then make marks along the binding edge of the door, allowing for a nice, even ⅛-inch final gap. Starting with the bottom hinge, tap out the hinge pins with a hammer and screwdriver. Support the door on shims, books, one foot, or get your helper to balance it for you. Once you've removed the hinge pins, lift the door off the hinge sleeves and lay it on a steady work surface.

Draw a straight line that tapers between the marks you made earlier. If you have a veneered door, score the veneer first with a utility knife to prevent tear-out. Trim the excess material

 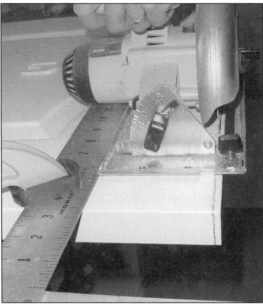

Marking the door while it is still hanging in the frame.   Using a straightedge to guide the saw accurately.

with a plane or saw. Reinstall the door. Test to see if that did the trick or if there are more edges that need to be planed.

Fixing doors is a cruel IQ test pitting you against the forces of a ruthless carpentry god. If you feel a sense of creeping despair, send your helper out for libations and load some Doritos into your tool belt. This is one battle you're going to win.

Squeak and Ye Shall Mind

Lubing up a squeaky hinge

Having houseguests can reveal some valuable insights about life. Maybe your list is similar to mine:

1. The steam from a kettle left boiling for twenty-five minutes while you're recounting an amusing anecdote to your guests can remove stubborn stains from the underside of kitchen cabinets and even stubborn paint.

2. A laundry load of wet table linen left sitting in the washing machine since the day before the guests arrived is not likely to smell "meadow fresh" when hastily dried and set on the table.

3. Using a lot of garlic in the food may cover the odor of mildewy napkins.

4. Sixteen cloves of garlic is probably too much for any one pasta dish.

5. Serving a muscular red wine may temper the odor of garlic.

6. Drinking cheap wine triggers many extra trips to the bathroom after bedtime.

7. Squeaky bathroom door hinges can keep the entire household awake most of the night.

Most of the items on my list are related to inherent character flaws, but one of them is completely fixable. Let's start with that, since fixing a personality is expensive and possibly hopeless.

Out, Darned Squeak

Squeaking door hinges may be noisy for several reasons, including bad paint jobs, corrosion, rust, wear and tear, or old lubricant that's become sticky. There are several ways to fix a squeaky hinge. You can try standing underneath the hinge, reaching up, and squirting a lubricant into it. Using this technique guarantees lubricant in your hair and eyebrows, running down your arm, down your leg, down the door, and onto the carpet. Depending on your personality, you may be unable to avoid this approach.

> Life is like a ride on a swinging pendulum. You keep expecting it to slow down and stop at a nice cozy spot, but the pendulum never rests. So the least you can do, like your mother always said, is try to have a pleasant facial expression.

TIPS

• Don't use cooking oil as a hinge lubricant. It works in a pinch but gets really sticky in about a month.

• Also, avoid using dry graphite powder as a hinge lubricant. Graphite tends to distribute fine black powder in a gentle mist all over everything, which is OK for an outdoor gate or a garage door, but not for indoors (unless you've decorated with a nightclub theme of black-on-black).

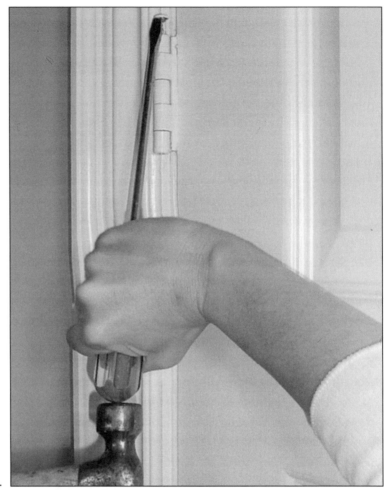

Using a hammer and screwdriver to remove the hinge pin.

A cleaner approach is to take the hinge pins out one at a time and work on them in sequence, replacing each one after you've cleaned and lubricated it. That way there will be at least one hinge in place at all times, so the door doesn't crash to the floor while you have your back turned.

Pin Up

To remove a hinge pin, place the tip of a nail on the underside of the hinge pin and then tap it with a hammer. This should force the hinge pin up and out. If your hinge is designed in such a way that the nail technique won't work, try sliding the tip of a slotted screwdriver under the head of the hinge pin and then whack the handle of the screwdriver with a hammer. Work from side to side on the head until there's enough of the pin showing that you can wrap your fingers or pliers around it and yank it out.

Now that you've got the hinge pin out, inspect it to see how badly corroded it is. If it's rusty or pitted on the surface, run steel wool over it until the surface is smooth and slightly glossy.

SAFETY ALERT!

- Whenever you use a hammer, wear your safety goggles.
- And avoid using plastic-handled screwdrivers for tapping (like I did in the photo); they can shatter.

Lube Job

Many people will tell you to lubricate your hinges with WD-40, but it's not a lubricant. Surprised? I know I was. The WD stands for Water Displacement. By displacing water from metal surfaces, WD-40 prevents rust and corrosion, but it's too light to work as a long-lasting lubricant.

By the way, the 40 in WD-40 stands for the number of attempts it took the lead scientist, Norm Larsen, to get the formula right. No wonder my pasta dish didn't work. It was GS-02-UO (Garlic Surprise, second attempt, uh-oh).

WD-40 is brilliant at cleaning off corrosion, degreasing surfaces, and preventing rust. But since it was never intended as a lubricant, you'll need to add something to the hinges after you've cleaned them with WD-40, or they'll be squeaking again in no time.

Many people swear by rubbing the hinge pin on the surface of a candle to coat it with a long-lasting waxy layer. My favorite is motorcycle-chain lubricant, which is so thorough you can even skip the WD-40. Castrol Chainlube, for example, is formulated to clean, penetrate, and protect, just like WD-40. But it goes one step further. It lubricates. So this adds an antiwear capability. Plus it's formulated to be non-drip, so no disastrous spot-removal emergencies.

Motorcycle-chain lubricant was developed to penetrate deeply into metal for a long-lasting, slippery coating that won't wear off or be affected by changes in temperature and humidity. As a last resort you can use petroleum jelly. It tends to collect dust and dirt, but it will otherwise provide long-wearing, non-drippy service. (Clean the hinge pins first with WD-40, then slather on the petroleum jelly and work the hinge pin up and down and up and down to distribute the lubricant. Ask any married person for pointers.)

May your next experience with houseguests be both garlic-neutral and squeak-free.

Unhinged!

Tuning up Euro hinges

> When you spend time alone, quietly working away at something, your individuality begins to assert itself. The renowned actress Tallulah Bankhead said, "Nobody can be exactly like me. Even I have trouble doing it."

If you've recently had a frustrating encounter with a bureaucrat, here's a suggestion: Simply adjust your kitchen cabinet hinges so the doors are properly aligned. This is the only human undertaking that is more difficult than trying to get information from a bureaucrat. Adjusting your hinges will teach you that there are worse things in life. Like "minor" home maintenance chores.

Not every style of hinge is annoying, so yours may not count. But if you have European-style hinges, where the cabinet door is hinged directly to the inside wall of the cabinet by a complex-looking mechanism, then, oh baby, you're the perfect candidate for this exasperating exercise.

For clarification, European hinges are fitted with several screws (sometimes hidden underneath a removable decora-

Euro hinge.

tive nameplate). By making subtle adjustments to those screws, you can tune up doors that may be hanging in weird ways. For example:

1. The doors pop forward and remain slightly open.
2. The bottom edges of the doors don't line up.
3. The doors are tilted.
4. On a double-door cabinet, there is a huge gap between the doors when they're closed.
5. Or the opposite: The doors are too close together and they rub against each other.

Count the number of screws on one of your hinges. Multiply this number by twenty-five to calculate your diastolic blood pressure by the time you're finished. Still want to continue? OK, but don't say I didn't warn you.

There are dozens of brands of Euro hinges. The designs vary and so do the screw positions. The important thing to remember is that each screw performs its own job, and your task is to guess what that job might be. Possibilities are:

An attitude adjustment.

1. The screw secures the hinge to the door or cabinet frame.
2. The screw adjusts the cabinet doors up or down. (The same screw may be doing double duty securing the hinge to the door or frame.)
3. The screw secures the hinge assembly to the brackets or baseplate. This particular screw also adjusts the plane of the door (once it's in closed position) either closer to or farther from the front plane of the cabinet.
4. The screw adjusts the doors left or right. This is the single factor that makes Euro hinges so popular. Even if the cabinet isn't remotely square you can tilt the doors to make them look square. Adjusting one hinge tilts the door. Adjusting both the top and bottom hinge shifts the entire door left or right.

If you can't guess the function of a screw merely by looking at it, then gird your loins. We're going in. You'll need a Phillips screwdriver, the kind with the X-shaped business end.

This stage of the process is aptly named "trial and error," although in the *ToolGirl Dictionary of Home Repair Slang*, it shows up variously as "fix and fail," "test and swear," or "check and chuck." If you're a hotheaded tool-thrower, make sure you offset aggravation with a soothing CD like *Bullfrogs at Dusk* or *Gaelic Harp Stylings of the Murdoch Sisters*.

Two hints: First, the back screw is usually the one that moves the door in or out and locks the door in place. You should see a channel in the hinge arm that allows the hinge to slide in or out. Loosen the screw, slide the hinge a little, then retighten the screw. Check the door, then readjust, *ad curseum*, until it's right. Second, the front screw usually moves the door left or right. Turning the screw clockwise moves the door one way; counterclockwise moves it the other way. Try to see which way the door moves. Sometimes it's not obvious which way it went until you close the door.

Adjusting hinges takes stamina and persistence. Once you're done, you'll understand what it feels like to have your blood boil. But your doors will be straight. And that's a priority we can all proudly share.

A Dab'll Do Ya

Minimalist wall repairs

They say that when you're about to die, your whole life flashes before you. If your life has included some bad repair jobs, having to watch yourself botch them all over again could finish you right off. Would we die anyway, or is the process of reviewing heinous DIY moments the actual cause of death?

Perhaps I can comment on this. As the former owner of a short-circuiting toaster, I've had several chances to review my life. I can confirm that a flashback of an ugly wall-patch job was enough to make me want to "quit this mortal coil" (a phrase attributed to Shakespeare after he attempted a fridge repair).

So let me share my tricks for fixing small holes in walls. I'm talking specifically about tiny screw holes and nail punctures left by previous installations of pictures, blinds, curtain rods, bookshelf brackets, etc. You can completely change the energy of a room by fixing these holes, especially if they're at eye level. If you've recently moved into a house or apartment that's got lots of these little perforations, you can easily disguise them, turning a pockmarked wall into a flawless background for exhibiting your collection of blister-packed Hot Wheels.

Have you ever noticed that when you finish a repair you feel serene and quiet? Kind of like after you give blood and they hold up that little red bag at the end and smile at you. That's when you know you've done something good. And if you still need proof, they give you a cookie.

TIPS

- Remember, paint dries a shade darker than it appears when it's still wet. Rule of thumb: One dab of paint that's even close to the existing paint color will disappear into the background of the wall, so don't worry it to death if you can't get the exact shade you want. However, err in the direction of darker when you're spot-painting a dark wall, and lighter when you're trying to match a light-colored wall.

Step 2: Filling the hole with a tiny amount of filler.

Texture Lecture

Simple patch jobs can turn into total remodels if you lack restraint. For example, when you use a putty knife or trowel to apply spackle or drywall compound, you can't help building up texture on the surface of the wall surrounding the hole. That texture is subtly different from the existing wall surface, and the discrepancy is almost impossible to fix later. Even under several coats of paint you'll still see the patch.

So rather than executing big, obvious patches, a more subtle approach is to try to disguise the hole. Camouflaging creates less mess and is way less noticeable than feathering spackle in ever-widening circles in the vague hope that the more trouble you go to, the better the results will be.

Steps

1. Carefully study the hole. If the nail was removed sloppily, it may have torn or lifted the paper sheathing on the drywall underneath the paint. Clean up the hole by cutting the loose paper edges back with a sharp knife. Remember, the idea is to keep the hole *small*, not to dig a strip mine. If you have an enthusiastic nature and don't trust yourself with the knife, you can instead press the paper back into the hole using a dull, convex object like the end of a pen. Push the edges gently back into line with the plane of the wall so they don't protrude at all.

2. Fill each hole with a tiny dab of spackle or drywall compound. Use a toothpick or the tip of a small knife (artist's palette knives are great) to apply a very refined amount of compound to the hole. Scrape it flush with the surface of the wall. It may shrink a bit as it dries, so you might need to repeat this step. If you smear any compound on the surrounding wall, wipe the excess away with a moistened Q-Tip so no residue remains on the wall surface around the edges of the hole.

3. When the patching material is fully cured, use a fine artist's brush to dab it lightly with a bit of the original paint color. All evidence of the hole instantly disappears. You can look away and look back and you won't be able to find it. Sweet.

Adding the final touch.

4. If you don't have any of the original paint, you can blend various shades of artist's acrylics into a base tint of white wall paint. (Make sure to match the base's gloss level with that of the paint you're trying to match.) Add and blend colors of acrylic paint until you get a shade that's close enough to work. To match a dark color of paint, start with a clear base rather than a white base. (A small tub of clear artist's acrylic medium is great to have on hand for darks.)
5. If you're totally inexperienced with blending colors, you will immediately achieve a vast range of browns, but no blues, pinks, greens, or yellows. This is a sign from the paint gods that you need to pick up a color wheel from the paint shop or art store. The wheel never lies.

This is the kind of repair that puts the "nit" in humanity, but if my opening theory is correct, you'll live longer.

2 OUTDOOR MAINTENANCE

A superior fix-it person always has a devious streak. Some of us are very talented in this department. How about you? Take this simple quiz to score your DIY aptitude:

1. When you were a kid, did you ever get together with other kids and set off firecrackers *not* on the Fourth of July, build illicit forts in Old Man Johnson's back field, or stand around in a circle and then simultaneously drop your shorts and observe each other's personal regions?

2. When confronted by your parents with evidence of wrongdoing, was your position usually, "It wasn't me. It was that hellion next door, Richard Campbell."

If you answered yes to either of these questions, you already possess classic DIY flair. You're apt to go looking for trouble, but you seldom work alone, meaning there's no danger of having to accept total responsibility for the outcome. There are lots of people just like us. We recognize each other at parties. We're the ones who hang around the kitchen trying to figure out how the cappuccino machine works, and after the explosion we leave quietly through the back door without our coats. We have creativity, but it's *unconventional* creativity.

We'll probably never get rich with our kind of creativity, but we're important to society in other ways. For example, if it weren't for us, manufacturers wouldn't have to print "Not to be put over head" on plastic bags, and hardware stores wouldn't have a no-returns policy on cracked toilets.

We like finding new ways to do things — preferably hard ways that start with enormous difficulty and end with hiding. We have improvising natures. We don't exactly use creative license; it's more of a creative subpoena, because we can't help what we do. Just use common sense. Remember the DIY motto: "The gene pool is crowded. Don't try anything that could jeopardize your place in the shallow end near the cute lifeguard."

Keeping Your Tools Up

Maintaining garden implements

It's hard to explain why I was sharpening my mother's garden tools in the back of my van in the parking lot of a strip mall, but I was. It's even harder to explain how my hand slipped, causing a hoe to violate my index finger, but it probably had something to do with being hopped up on spring hormones.

Now that I'm back home, the big gauze bandage on my finger takes up three letters on the computer keyboard, causing trouble when I type the words "tfsdtrhj" or "ffoisk." So it is with humility that I offer the following tips on getting your garden tools in shape for spring.

It was Aristotle who said, "The hardest victory is victory over self." But clearly, victory over a gardening tool is way harder. Aristotle was a smart guy, but I'm guessing he had to make up a lot of those lofty statements because he just wasn't handy.

Owie!

TIPS

• When you're sharpening, it is best to clamp the tool securely in a vise rather than hold it, however stalwartly, between your thighs.

• If you own a Dremel rotary tool, you can load it up with a stone grinding bit and cut your sharpening time to a fraction.

• Shovels and hoes should only be sharpened on one side, but edging tools, axes, hatchets, and trowels can be sharpened on both sides.

Rusting Out All Over

Rust buildup causes drag on the blades of shovels, trowels, hoes, and edging tools, making it harder to push the tool through soil. This can totally put you off gardening if the sight of halved worms isn't doing that already.

You can usually remove rust with a combined assault of wire brush, sandpaper, penetrating oil, and steel wool. However, the hoe I was working on was so rusty that I was completely covered in red dust after twenty minutes of hand sanding, and there was still no sign of shiny steel. So I fired up my electric sander and buffed the living daylights out of that baby. When I got down to silvery steel, it was sharpening time.

File and Error

A gardening tool's blade should be sharp enough to cut through dirt as though it were young cheese. This makes chores go faster so you arrive sooner at the best part of gardening: beer.

You'll need a flat "bastard" file or "mill" file, a standard metal file that removes metal slowly but effectively. They cut in one direction only, so you have to use one-way strokes.

Make sure the tool is properly secured, preferably with a clamp or vise, so that the blade is facing up. Using both hands to hold the file, push away from your body to make long, smooth strokes down and sidewise across the blade in a sort of sliding motion. The double-milled face of the file cuts most aggressively, so use it to form the initial edge, then tidy it up with the single-milled face.

Try to copy the tool's original bevel. In most cases, you should aim for a bevel between forty and seventy-five degrees. If the bevel is too sharp, the edge will bend and chip when it strikes roots or rocks. Work until you have a consistent, smooth, shiny edge along the entire blade. Sometimes there are dings and pits in the edge, so it may take some work. Enjoy it. This investment will make your whole summer easier.

When you're done, spray the whole blade with Pam or wipe on light machine oil to prevent rust from getting started again.

A freshly sharpened edger, some files, sandpaper, and steel wool.

Love Handles

To prevent wooden tool handles from splitting, drying, and distributing slivers, rub the gripping areas with boiled linseed oil once each spring. (You buy the linseed oil already boiled; you don't have to boil it yourself. I'll only make that mistake once.)

Barrows of Fun

Wheelbarrows get rusty and eventually develop holes in their bottoms. You can avoid wheelbarrow burnout by sanding out rusty spots and recoating the entire wheelbarrow surface with rustproof spray paint in a fashionable shade of dirt brown.

Swell Done

If you've got loose tools, there is relief. When a tool's head has separated or become loose on a wooden handle, soak the tool's neck in a tray or bucket of antifreeze overnight. Make sure the antifreeze covers the section where the wooden handle joins the metal head. The antifreeze penetrates the wood fibers, swelling them, and then holds them in the new shape so that the head no longer wobbles.

Finally, if you're going to perform maintenance procedures on your garden tools, don't rush. If you must attempt sharpening a hoe in the back of your van, at least get the bumper sticker that reads, "If this van's a-rockin', call an ambulance."

Stop and Smell the Hoses

Repairing hose couplings

Sometimes you drive over the end of your hose and squash the coupling. You're not aiming for it; you just get lucky. The downside is that now it's harder to drink from. The upside is that the crushed coupling makes it unnecessary to hold your thumb over the end when hosing down relatives.

If you're like me, a ruined hose is a semiannual event. More than that, it's a great excuse to go to the hardware store. In that tool-filled haven, the mingled scents of wood, rubber, and fertilizer cause the body to produce "repairamones." People with elevated repairamone levels often find romance in the hardware store. They feel an immediate sense of recognition, even before they discover that they both have a broken part. In mystical circles, they are called Toolmates. But enough of legend; we're fixing a hose here.

A dirty mind should occasionally be rinsed.

Whoever said that home repair is the underbelly of home ownership just wasn't being fair to underbellies. Underbellies are one of the most lovable parts of many mammals. Go ahead, take a peek at your own underbelly. That warm little spot houses the future of the species, and if that doesn't scare you, you're a perfect candidate for home ownership.

Tools
Utility knife, measuring tape, screwdriver, clamp

Materials
Replacement coupling, pail of hot water, clear silicone sealant

Steps
1. Observe the attributes of the damaged hose coupling, which is either male or female. If it is female, it is threaded on the inside surface so that it firmly grips the male's ridges. If it is male, it is threaded on the outside and designed to fit

TIPS

• Replacement fittings are usually brass or high-impact plastic. The plastic ones are great because they're relatively leak-proof and cooperative. The brass ones are more expensive, hard to force into place, and tend to leak because they come with a metal hose clamp that can be difficult to tighten effectively.

• If your hose has a duct-taped section in the middle where it's leaking, you can try to get another season out of it, or you can fix it right now. The clamps and procedures are almost identical for inserting a "union," which fixes a leak in the center of a hose. With your newfound know-how, you can install a union in minutes and still be done by beer-thirty.

beautifully inside the female. If you buy the wrong-sized or wrong-sexed replacement piece, you'll never be a hose breeder. Know your parts.

2. With a utility knife, sever the damaged coupling from your hose. Pocket the squished bit for later reference in the hardware store. Now look at the cross-sectional view of your remaining hose and measure the interior diameter. The replacement coupling must fit the internal diameter of your hose, so this is an important measurement. Replacement couplings come in several sizes to match hose diameters: ½-inch, ⅝-inch, ¾-inch, and universal. "Universal" is a nice word meaning "won't fit any existing hose."

3. Go to your hardware store and survey the array of hose connectors, fittings, and couplings. Choose the appropriate size and sex. If you didn't bring your damaged coupling, by now you may have forgotten exactly which shape and size it was. Many bad guesses are made at this crucial point. If you get home with a nice new male but find the fit is wrong or, worse, that you already had a male at home, it's embarrassing to correct. Because of these errors in judgment many people have extra couplings in strange places.

4. With the correctly chosen replacement part in hand, return home. Fill a pail with hot water and soak the cut-off end of your hose in it. This will soften it so it's able to accept the width of the shaft you will soon be inserting into it.

5. Loosen the screws on the clamp, and slide it around the hose-end so it is ready to be tightened.

6. Now for the best part: Coat the shaft of the replacement connector with clear silicone sealant. Holding the shaft in one hand and the softened hose in the other, push the lubricated length of the shaft into the opening. Once it is in as far as it will go, tighten the clamp with a screwdriver.

The Long and Short of It

The fascinating world of extension cords

If you're like me, and I know I am, your extension cords are patched every couple of feet with black electrician's tape. Is this safe? No. Is there a way to make it safe? Sure. Use the cord to reweave your patio furniture.

Maybe you've scarred your extension cord by running over it with your lawn mower, or you may have yanked on it

When you're thoroughly engrossed in fixing something, insignificant problems drop away. You just stop worrying about what to cook for dinner, or why bird poo is white, or who invented thong underwear.

Chairman of the cord.

TIPS

• If you have trouble remembering the counter-intuitive American Wire Gauge System, use this handy comparison: When you habitually consume a high number of calories, you are likely to state your weight as being less than it actually is. It's the same with extension cords: the higher the voltage they transport, the more modest they are about it.

• Use your elbow and hand to wind your extension cord in a figure-eight pattern so that your coil will unwind next time without tangling.

so many times that the insulation is fractured and frayed where the cord disappears into the plug. Instead of replacing the entire cord, you can just install a new cord cap (plug). This is a cinch — assuming you've unplugged the cord at the outlet.

Quick Fix

1. Buy a replacement plug (either male or female, depending on which end of the cord you're repairing) that's rated to match the amperage of your extension cord. If in doubt, cut off the plug and take it with you to the hardware store.

2. If you haven't already done it, cut the plug off using wire cutters or a sharp knife.

Step 2: Cutting off the frayed plug.

3. Carefully cut the outer cable jacket to reveal an inch of each of the wires: black, white, and green.

4. Cut away the fibers that compose the filling material.

5. From each of the three wires, strip a half inch of insulation.

6. Twist the exposed strands of wire to keep them from fraying.

7. Slide the plastic housing onto the cord. (I usually forget this step in my hurry to get to the screwing.)

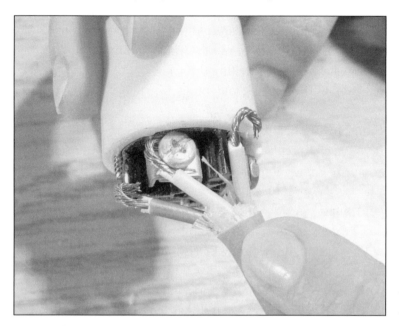

Step 8: Hooking the wires over the screw terminal in a clockwise direction.

Step 9: Tightening up the housing plug. Look for a tab that locks into a corresponding slot; otherwise, it won't go back together.

SAFETY ALERT!

• Do not use extension cords that are cut or damaged. Touching even a single exposed strand of wire can give you a nasty electric shock or burn.

• If you're going to use an extension cord to power two or more appliances, you should add together the wattage rating for all the appliances used on the cord. The total of those wattage ratings will help you determine which gauge size you will need.

8. Attach the wires in exactly the following order: green (ground) wire to the green terminal, black wire to the brass screw terminal, and white wire to the silver terminal.

Wrap the copper wire around the screw terminals in a clockwise direction to prevent it from slipping off the terminal as you're tightening the screw.

9. Close up the housing and, bingo, you're back in the game.

Gauge before Beauty

If you need to replace an extension cord, know your options. Some are longer, some are thicker; which matters most? Choosing is an intensely personal matter. Here are some guidelines:

The copper wires that are hidden inside a heavy-duty, outdoor-rated, three-prong extension cord come in a range of gauges (diameters). You can learn to use the word "gauge" with confident abandon by understanding that the larger the wire, the smaller the gauge number. This system is called the American Wire Gauge System and was devised many years ago by some illogical nutbar; now we all have to live with it.

Another thing to know about gauge is that the smaller the gauge number, the more current the cord can carry. For instance, the fatter wires in a ten-gauge cord can power higher wattage appliances than the skinnier wires in a sixteen-gauge cord.

Length or Width?

The heavier your appliance's demand for current, the lower the cord's gauge should be, so know your user profile. You'll need a lower gauge cord for equipment that works against a heavy load, like hammer drills boring into concrete, or electric lawn mowers cutting through extension cords.

All appliances are stamped with how much wattage is consumed when operated, and the manual might even suggest what length and gauge of cord to use with your power tool or appliance. Some appliances indicate power usage in amps rather than watts. Here's a high-school physics tip: If your appliance uses 5 amps at 125 volts, then its wattage rating is 625 W (5×125).

You also have to consider the cord length. The farther you get from the electrical outlet, the less current reaches the motor of your appliance, because of resistance over the length of the cord. For example, I once tried to power a fridge on a movie set with a hundred-foot extension cord. The fridge was supposed to be full of cold drinks for the crew, but nothing in that fridge got cold. Ever. It was as if the fridge was trying to suck current through a tiny straw and just couldn't get enough. We dragged the fridge closer to the outlet, installed a shorter, lower gauge cord, and the drinks got cold.

Burning for It

Trouble can start when you hook two or three shorter cords together to make the length you need. Not only does current get lost through resistance over the length of the combined cords, but it also drops a little every time the current hits another plug connection. If the motor doesn't get enough current, your appliance or power tool may run for a while and then burn out, or it may just hum but not actually engage, making you think you need an expensive repair when in fact you only need a lower gauge and/or shorter extension cord.

Moist and Dangerous

Why bother with outdoor caulking?

A Chinese proverb says, "With time and patience, the mulberry leaf becomes a silk gown." That mulberry leaf spends a long time in the silkworm's digestive tract, though. This gives fresh meaning to the phrase "seeing the light at the end of the tunnel."

You know how there's always someone telling you what *not* to do, and that just makes you want to do it? For example, printed on Sharpie permanent markers is the instruction "Not for letter writing." Well, when I'm feeling wild, I pick up a Sharpie and I write a letter. What a rush.

But back to rules. I don't always trust the intelligence of rule-makers. I want to know *why* they made up a particular rule. One way to find out is to write polite letters (using a Sharpie), asking for explanations and case studies. A quicker way that requires no postage is simply to break the rule and see what happens. This frequently gets me into extreme learning experiences known as trouble.

For instance, the reason they tell you not to insert the Reddi-wip nozzle directly into your mouth is because Reddi-wip is stored under tremendous pressure and when you depress the trigger, it packs your nasogastric chambers in less than three milliseconds. This makes it difficult to start a conversation, particularly if your opening line is "Help, I can't breathe," although in thorny social situations this could be just the icebreaker everyone needs.

There are some rules that shouldn't be challenged, and they usually include the word "moisture." Rules about moisture are part of human life from an early age:

Kindergarten: Do not allow moisture to penetrate your clothing. Raise your hand and the teacher will permit egress to the restroom.

Sixth Grade: Do not allow moisture to penetrate clothing under your arms. If moisture egresses into your clothing, do not raise your hand under any circumstances.

High School: Do not do anything that creates moisture of any kind. Anywhere. Ever. Especially in a vehicle.

Adulthood: Moisture in the form of fermented beverages is permissible except when stranded in a remote location with an attractive co-worker, in which case revert to Moisture Rules for High School.

Retirement: Do not allow moisture to penetrate your joints. Move to Florida.

Old Age: Do not allow moisture to penetrate your clothing.

The one moisture rule that everyone breaks at one time or another is this: Do not allow moisture to penetrate your dwelling. Want to know why that rule was made up? Let me explain. It's a size thing. Even the smallest crack in the exterior surface of your home is thousands of times bigger than a water molecule. And water molecules, through the miracle of "capillary action," never come alone. They bring chains of their friends, all bunched together like teenagers in a mall.

Water molecules are natural risk-takers and will explore any available cranny. Some say they have an exaggerated sense of immortality, since the worst thing that can happen to them is that they get vaporized and beamed up to rejoin the Water Cycle. That would make anyone cocky.

In the fall, water molecules are rowdy and delinquent, hurling themselves against buildings in bursts of wind-driven rain. They dash themselves deep into cracks in search of spelunking opportunities.

Then our tale turns ugly, because those molecules don't always evaporate before the cold weather sets in. Instead, they find themselves freezing and expanding into crystal gigantisms

TIPS

• If you live in a newer home and your basement walls are cinder block or concrete, you can paint them with newly available latex-based waterproof paint to seal the walls permanently against moisture leakage.

• If you never want to do exterior caulking again, save up and buy "elas-tomeric" caulk. It lasts fifty years, fills joints as wide as a half inch, and is still paintable. It's also extremely flexible through freeze/thaw cycles.

• Take the old stuff out first; you'll get a better seal.

• Cocktail conversation: The father of modern caulks was Robert Dicks.

that are too big for the crack they're stuck in. So, in their "we don't stop for nobody" tradition, water molecules just shoulder the crack open a bit and enjoy their glorious new physique.

After crack-trapped water goes through the freeze-and-thaw cycle a few times in fall, that crack may have deepened enough to allow moisture to seep right into your framing,

Tracking a crack.

locking dampness into the walls and creating desirable digs for mildew spores, carpenter ants, and termites.

So fall is the time of year to scrutinize your foundation, windows, doors, and trim. If existing caulking is in bad shape, either scrape it off and start fresh, or augment the existing stuff using a good acrylic-latex exterior caulk that's guaranteed for at least twenty-five years.

Caulking has come a long way in the last decade. Today's caulks no longer ossify, fail, pull away from joint surfaces, shrink, or curl; they're incredibly durable and actually have lots of elasticity to expand and contract as the temperature changes. DAP Alex Plus is one of my favorites. It's available in different colors: taupe, grey, white, cream, tan, dark brown, etc., and it's also paintable.

If you hate caulking guns, try Loctite Press and Seal, a pressurized tube of high-grade, paintable caulk with an easy-action built-in trigger.

Before you start caulking, fill a small container with warm water mixed with a few drops of dishwashing soap. After you apply a bead of caulking, moisten your fingertip in the soapy solution, and then smooth the caulk in a long, even stroke. Very Zen. And the soapy water prevents the caulk from sticking to your finger. Make sure you press firmly so the caulk adheres to both sides of the joint you're filling. And always smooth the fresh bead within a few minutes of applying it or it will start to skin over and you'll make a big mess. I usually start out wearing latex gloves, but once the fingers get all bonded together I ditch 'em and work with naked tips.

If caulk doesn't solve your moisture problems, check to see if the aluminum siding on your home is loose, broken, or missing. Fix the damaged area by replacing it with a new piece of siding. To make the new piece stick, run a bead of silicone sealant around the entire perimeter on the wrong

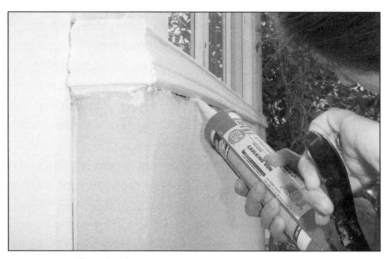

Be sure to caulk under the trim.

side of the patch, and then press it into position. Tape it there and leave it for at least an hour while the sealant sets up.

If none of these solutions work, your house may have drainage issues below ground level (e.g., an encroaching water table or underground spring). This requires excavation, waterproofing, and luck — the kind of luck you may not have. So hire a professional. But when you have an acute situation with water pouring through your basement walls during a dinner party, emergency tactics are necessary.

Applying hydraulic cement to leaks or cracks on the interior side of foundation walls is dead easy and will stop an active leak in its tracks. Widen your cracks first with a cold chisel, undercutting the edges. (Cement adheres to an under-cut opening better than it sticks to a V-shaped trench.) Mix a small batch of hydraulic cement to the consistency of icing, and then trowel it into the crevice. Remember, a job well done is a job that's never over. That makes home repair about as close to immortality as some of us will ever get, so enjoy it.

If It's Not One Thing, It's a Gutter

Gutter maintenance

I've matured, and so can you. This season I've cleaned out my gutters in a timely manner, as beer is my witness.

Let me share my secret for gutter gusto. I got in touch with the ancient power of irritability. When you're irritated, you're in a metabolically superior state. You're ready for physical and emotional challenges; in fact, you're begging for them. Being irritated is an opportunity to channel vigor into stuff you've been putting off, like scooping out fetid gutters.

Remember, timing is essential. Don't ruin a great mood with a reeking, dirty project like gutter maintenance. Wait until you're already testy. Only then are you physiologically stoked for the job. Also, don't wait for a nice day. The worse the weather, the more foul your mood will be, and the greater the odds that you'll complete the job in record time.

Finally, eat something that leaves you bloated, put on ill-fitting clothes that accentuate bulgy spots, and wear tight shoes over your itchiest socks. Feel the rebirth of your inner hellcat.

Give Inky Dinky What For

Downspouts get compacted with rotting leaves. Give your downspouts a high colonic. Set the hose nozzle on Stun, insert your arm as far up as it will go, and blast repeatedly into the bottom end of the downspout, continuing until there is a soggy expulsion of clumpy crud. You are utterly soaked by now, and the sleeve of your shirt looks (and possibly smells) like you've been delivering calves. Press on. It's just starting to get good.

It was Maltbie D. Babcock who said, "Our business in life is not to get ahead of other people, but to get ahead of ourselves." He was right, because if you don't stay ahead of yourself when you're doing maintenance, you end up beside yourself. And one of you is going to be cranky.

TIPS

• If your downspouts have multiple elbows or angles, especially near the bottom, remove the bent portions and feed the hose into the main downspout to attack the clogs more directly.

Yuck!

Now climb a ladder with the hose and try running some water into the top of the downspout. If it's still backing up, you have more clogs. Blast the top opening of the downspout with your hose. If you get a faceful of backspray, try packing rags around the hose so that doesn't happen again. If repeated blasts fail to clear the clog, resort to a drain auger or "snake," a suitably annoying appliance that almost never works well.

Gutter Fingers

Once the downspouts are cleared, proceed with scooping the guck out of the gutters, moving the ladder along as you progress. Use a garden trowel for heavy sludge. As you work, check for loose spikes or brackets, the fasteners that hold the gutter in place. Some repair manuals recommend marking trouble spots on the outside of the gutter with colored chalk so you can find the problem areas later, when you're ready to repair them, which might be never, so you may as well use permanent marker.

Once the gutters are clear, flood them with water from the hose and watch for leaks. Sometimes gaps form between sections of gutters, especially at corners. Use gutter sealant to patch holes and seal open joints. Make sure you buy the correct type of sealant; gutters are made from vinyl, aluminum, or galvanized metal, and each material requires a different sealant.

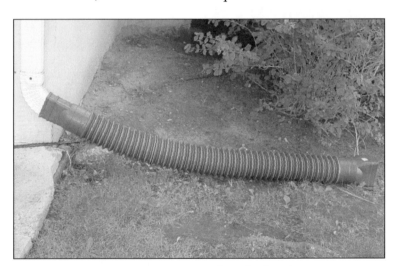

Downspout extensions carry water away from the foundation.

Starting from Patch

Patch any holes by cleaning the area with rubbing alcohol or acetone. Then smear gutter sealant around the hole. Lay a piece of fiberglass mesh or metal bug screen over the hole. Coat the whole patch with several layers of gutter sealant.

Remember, the whole point of this irritating ordeal is to protect your foundation. The water collected by an average roof in summer is enough to fill several swimming pools. If your downspouts are depositing rainwater right beside your foundation, buy downspout extensions so you can divert water at least six feet away from your foundation. End of lecture. I was only trying to keep you irritated. It's for your own good, hothead.

Foam Is Where the Heart Is

Home security in a can

The great Samuel Johnson said that few things are impossible with diligence and skill. But most people are born with one or the other, not both, so you have to learn which one you've got and develop the other. Or find someone else who has it and suck him or her into working with you.

When you wake up at 4 AM hearing something scratching, do you assume it's a nearby relative who should bathe more often? This is how denial can lead to your home being a target for local rodents searching for climate-controlled lodgings. There's an old saying, "When nights get nippy, rodents get an address." Every fall, the average mouse deserts his tiny, frigid grass hut under the snow to mooch off a fellow mammal's heating bill.

Starting around October, rodents become motivated and creative. A mouse can squeeze through a quarter-inch slit in a wall. A rat can reliably shimmy through an opening the size of a quarter. Some rodents enter through gaps surrounding cable, conduit, or pipes. Cracks in your foundation, mortar that needs patching, holes in siding (or pieces missing entirely) are other portals for furry hooligans.

And once they're inside, they high-five each other along freeways between floors, up and down pipes, under sinks, inside walls, between cupboards, through drawers, and behind appliances. Here's something else to watch out for: once they're warm and cozy, they relax. They let down their emotional guard and throw wild mouse parties that lead to fertility accidents. So allowing rodents to enter your home means condoning promiscuity, and we all remember the health class about that.

How can you tell if rodents are setting up camp in your home? You may recently have said one of the following tell-tale sentences: "Hey, honey, the stupid cat is staring at the basement ceiling again," or "OK, who spilled all the little black seeds in the pantry?" or "Whoa, this bar of soap had corners last night, and now it's round. Must be the humidity."

Keeping rodents out of the house in the first place is easier than getting them to leave once they're inside. The traditional way to stop rodents from entering your domicile is to stuff steel wool into visible cracks and holes. Rodents don't like chewing steel wool; it hurts their fillings. Despite this, they often manage to muscle their way through, so it's not a reliable barrier. Fortunately, nature has recently given us an alternative, with some help from giant chemical corporations. I'm talking about expanding foam sealant and lots of it.

There are two types of expanding foam sealant: polyurethane products and latex-based products. Both types fill gaps and holes that are too large to pack with caulking. Polyurethane foam cures to a rigid but porous texture, similar to an ossified cheese puff, and can be sculpted (with a bread knife) into a suitable shape. Latex foam cures to a spongy non-sculptable texture, but while it is still setting up it can be tooled, shaped, or molded, giving you lots of texturing options. Both latex and polyurethane foams stick to almost

TIPS

• Manufacturers always print a cryptic cautionary note on the label: "Once the foam has cured, no known chemical on this planet will dissolve it. Remove by sanding." If the foam is on your skin, good luck with the sanding part. I'm still smarting.

Ready for foam.

anything, including wood, aluminum, masonry, galvanized steel, plastic, rubber, drywall, glass, and, based on personal experience, skin.

Applying the polyurethane foam.

You can use expanding foam to rodent-proof your house. Fill cracks and holes under sinks and in and around your foundation, chimneys, and siding. Apart from discouraging rodents, foam has cosmetic potential. For example, my garage was missing a corner piece of aluminum siding. I tried to get a replacement corner, but they don't make them anymore, so I applied polyurethane foam and waited overnight for it to cure. Then I sculpted a new corner and painted it to match the siding. Oh, baby.

Here are more great things about expanding foam sealant:

1. Foam acts as a form-fitting barrier to the elements and has no nutritional value, so it doesn't attract insects or rodents.

2. Foam doesn't support the growth of mold or fungus in damp conditions.

3. It doesn't smell bad as you're using it, or after it's cured.

4. Many brands of foam are free of volatile organic compounds that pollute the environment. Look for the phrase "Low-VOC" or "No VOC" on the label.

5. Foam efficiently seals air leaks that compromise the energy efficiency of your home.

6. Foam sets up quickly, fills large voids, deadens sound, is airtight and water-resistant, and conforms to any shape as it expands.

7. Foam can (and should) be painted after it's fully cured to protect it from UV light, which causes discoloration and deterioration.

Trimming the cured foam with a bread knife.

If you haven't used expanding foam before, go with a low-expansion variety. (The label will indicate whether it's high- or low-expansion.) If you choose a high-expansion foam, use it with an extremely subtle touch. It expands 200 to 300 percent over a couple of hours. In other words, you only need to squirt in 35 to 50 percent of what you think you need. If you overdo it, you'll have pendulous globs of uncured foam spilling out of crevices, rolling down your walls, and spreading themselves around like a bad soprano. Uncured foam cleans up with acetone when it's still wet, but not easily, so don't let it get to that point.

Tamp Your Troubles Away

The empowering nature of potholes

Remember when your mother told you it isn't polite to grunt? She may not have told you about the times when it *is* polite. Like in some cases of childbirth or in all cases of moving a toilet. Your body needs an outlet for the pressure, and a grunt is way nicer than a prolapsed pyloric sphincter.

If you've ever dreamed of working on a road crew, don't be embarrassed. I have that dream too. But why torment yourself with this unfulfilled fantasy? You can make your dream come true in your very own driveway.

All you need to fix your own pothole is a bag of bitumen, a conveniently cooled and packaged version of the hot, smoking asphalt that those lucky road workers use. You can buy bags of room-temperature bitumen for about five bucks at the hardware store, and I think the word "party" comes to mind right away, doesn't it? Because strutting around with a bag of bitumen gives you some kind of social advantage over those who don't have bitumen or even know what it is.

I learned about the joys of asphalt repair when I was growing up in small-town Ontario. My dad would call the town to report a pothole on the street in front of our place. Twenty minutes later, when the works department *still* hadn't shown up, Dad would show the town a thing or two about promptness by hauling out the bitumen and filling that dang hole himself. Then he'd stand out there beside his master-piece, glowing, while the neighbors drifted over to admire the repair and ask bitumen-related questions. Life was sweet.

What my dad knew was that the sooner you fix a pothole, the better. Potholes cause awkward skateboard wipeouts, and I've got the scars to prove it. More importantly, if you don't repair driveway potholes, rainwater collects in them and seeps under the driveway surface. Once it permeates the underlying layer, the water eventually freezes once winter sets in and heaves the surface, further breaking down the asphalt surrounding the pothole.

TIPS

- Pick a nice hot day for this. Not only will you get a more realistic road-crew experience, but you'll also find the asphalt easier to work with when it's warm and soft.
- You can remove asphalt patch from your skin by rubbing toothpaste onto the stain.

Tools

Shovel, broom or whisk, dustpan and brush, shop vacuum (optional), hose and spray nozzle, heat gun or hair dryer (if needed)

Materials

Asphalt patch (bitumen), cinder block or longish piece of 4" × 4" lumber (for tamping)

Steps

1. Start by using a shovel to remove the bulk of the gravel and debris from the pothole. Keep going until you've reached the layer of compacted gravel that forms the foundation of the driveway. Break off and remove any loose chunks around the edge of the pothole too.

2. Next, use a broom or whisk, followed by a fine brush, to thoroughly rid the cavity of dust particles. If you have a shop vac, you can even vacuum the cavity. This may seem like overkill, but if you leave a layer of dust, the fresh asphalt will never get a good grip on the bottom layer, and your patch will just jostle around in the hole until it pops out like a wayward curling rock.

3. The final step in the preparation sequence requires blasting the hole with a quick, fine spray from a hose fitted with a nozzle. This wets down any remaining dust without saturating the cavity.

4. Split the bitumen bag open with a shovel and load into the hole to reach half an inch higher than the surrounding driveway surface. If the bitumen is stiff and chunky, soften it up with a heat gun or a hair dryer.

Tamping is primal. Grunt with abandon.

5. Tamp the loose bitumen down with a large hunk of lumber or the flat surface of a cinder block. Make sure you grunt. This puts you in touch with your inner hellion, but in a wholesome way. Pay special attention to tamping the edges of the patch; the more tightly compacted they are, the less likely they are to bust up under the usual driveway wear and tear.

6. Once you've tamped the patch into an invincible little plug, sweep some dust over the top of it to prevent it from sticking to tires and bare feet.

If tamping seems dangerously close to a primal ritual, you're on the right track. If, on the other hand, you feel tamping is too much work, simply drive over the patch a few times in your car and at least make the sound of a steamroller.

One Board Short of a Deck

Replacing funky lumber

One thing that can ruin your day is when your leg plunges thigh-deep through a board in your deck. At first you're shocked, but you move quickly into denial: "I can't have gained that much weight. It must be fluid retention."

The upside of plummeting through a rotten deck is that while you're healing, you have time to plan your repair. Although you now know of one rotten spot, other needy areas may not be so obvious. If your deck could speak, would it be rasping, "Hey, fatty, stand somewhere else. Can't you tell I'm spongy?" To avoid any more "breakthroughs," follow these steps to interpret what your deck is saying:

There have been days when I thought I was really making progress, only to be upended by some wayward piece of lumber. Hector Berlioz was right when he said, "Time is a great teacher, but unfortunately it kills all its pupils." So when people say they're killing time, I just laugh.

1. Drop a cheese puff on the deck. Squish it with your bare heel. If your heel absorbs most of the grease from the cheese puff, you should be using a foot moisturizer. However, if the board sucks up the cheese puff grease before your skin can, your deck needs to be sealed.
2. Pull out your pocket knife and press the tip of the blade into the wood. If it doesn't sink in at all, you need to sharpen your pocket knife. If it sinks in more than a quarter of an inch, or if the wood appears crumbly or powdery, you have dry rot and should think about replacing the funky board.
3. While you're thinking about replacing the board, drink beer for focus.

Identifying a rotten board using a pocket knife.

Moisture trapped between two wood surfaces (like between a board and the joist beneath it) makes a good home for fungi, which digests the wood. We call this dry rot. "Dry" is a misleading descriptor since rot is always caused by dampness. I can prove this by showing you my vegetable crisper.

When replacing a deck board, remember that demolition is more fun than construction; enjoy it fully. Wear safety glasses and something foxy. Looking your best helps maintain a good mood. Beer can only take you so far.

Steps

1. Start by using a claw hammer to pull the nails out of the board. The nail heads may break off. If this happens, use a "cat's paw" pry bar to really dig in under the head of the nail. The cat's paw tears up the surface of the board, but when demo is your goal, you don't care.

2. Once you've removed as many nails as possible, use a pry bar to lift the board, starting at one end. Grunt menacingly and twist the board with an attitude that says, "You and me are going to the dump together and only one of us is coming back."

3. Once you have the board out, inspect the joist that was supporting it. If there's evidence of minor rot but it's not too bad, remove any crumbly wood and then use a paintbrush to apply an antibug, anti-rot preparation such as Copper Green.

4. Replace the board with new lumber of the same variety as the rest of the decking. Fasten it in place using weather-resistant nails or screws.

5. Now seal the entire deck with a good water-based sealant. Don't forget this crucial step. Think of sealant like deodorant; once a year, whether you need it or not.

TIPS

• To age a new piece of lumber so it blends in with the older boards, brush tea onto the board. Let it dry. Then give it a coat of iron acetate, which you make by soaking a wad of steel wool for two days in a cup of vinegar mixed with one quart of water. The resulting iron acetate solution brushed onto the tea-stained lumber will interact with the tannins in the tea, turning the wood a dark silvery color.

• A nontoxic but effective mixture for cleaning off a mildewy deck is made by mixing three parts hot water to one part salt.

SAFETY ALERT!

• Antibug and anti-rot preparations are highly toxic—always wear protective clothing and gloves.

Once More with Sealing

Protecting pressure-treated wood

It was one of those weeks when I'd been feeling pudgy and out of shape. I knew that sometimes you can appear slimmer by dressing in black. So I dressed in black a lot. I thought it made me look foxy. Then someone said, "Jeez, you look tired." This from someone who usually says, "Whoa! Put on a few pounds lately?" so I felt I still had the upper hand.

Two negatives make a positive. So combining cranky, sweaty exercise with dirty, irritating chores will pay off in cheerfulness, and I've got just the galling, irksome task for you.

When it comes to maintaining a dwelling, more people are wrong about one thing: maintaining pressure-treated decks. Pressure-treated wood is bug- and decay-resistant, and it lasts approximately forty years before it decays significantly. However, it's *not* resistant to rain, sun, heat, freezing, and thawing. Many people don't realize this and never waterproof their decks.

Wood, whether treated or untreated, is like a sponge. It swells when wet and shrinks when dry. Unprotected, it discolors, cracks, splits, warps, twists, cups, splinters, and heaves. If you don't want a faded, rough, uninviting deck surface (and splinters in important body parts), you need to protect your pressure-treated wood from the elements. There are two products that will do this: clear, water-repellent sealer, and semitransparent stain. Water-repellent sealer can be applied at any time to old structures or brand-new ones. Semitransparent stain can be applied to older structures at any time, but it should be applied to new wood only after the surface has dried sufficiently.

New Decks

Sprinkle several drops of water on the deck's surface. If the water is immediately absorbed, the surface is ready to accept stain. If the water is not readily absorbed, check it again a couple of weeks later. Stain it as soon as it's dry.

Exterior wood should be sealed or stained once every year or two. I like to use a water-based sealant because it's less harmful to the environment, but the choice is up to you. Applying it with a pressurized garden sprayer is fastest, but I opt for the brush technique because it loosens my hamstrings.

Old Decks

Older decks need cleaning before you apply stain or sealant. You can buy deck-cleaning preparations or make your own. Some people use one cup of trisodium phosphate (TSP) in three quarts of water, but I don't recommend that because TSP is bad for water tables and lakes. Instead, try a mild organic detergent in water. If your deck has moss, algae, mildew, or mold growing on it, add salt to water in a ratio of three parts water to one part salt. Use a bristly push broom or scrub brush to scour the wood surface, and then rinse and let dry for forty-eight hours before applying sealant.

TIPS

• In new construction, freshly sawed ends of pressure-treated lumber expose the untreated insides of the board. Brush the raw ends with a wood preservative (e.g., Copper Green, a pesticide and preservative containing inorganic arsenic—the same stuff they use to pressure-treat wood).

A short attention span is no friend of proper sealant application.

Cleaning decks is a messy, infuriating job, so dedicate the ordeal to strengthening your quads with deep, controlled lunges behind the scrub broom. Then later you can cheerfully tan your shapely, rock-hard legs while lying on your silky smooth, freshly sealed deck.

To Screen the Impossible Screen

Vanquishing your screening meemies

They say that drinking alcoholic beverages kills brains cells. They also say that a glass of wine every day reduces the risk of heart disease. Plus, elderly people who have a daily drink are happier. So apparently, getting rid of surplus brain tissue means you arrive at old age healthier and happier. But why leave it until old age if you can get rid of that brain tissue by, say, forty-five? If I'd only started drinking sooner, I'd be happy and healthy by now.

Summer entertaining is great because everyone sits outside, so the spills don't have to be cleaned up. However, there are risks. For example, having people over for drinks is a leading cause of extroversion. And feeling jovial makes you a target for summer perils, like forgetting the screen door is closed when you're carrying a tray full of refreshments.

Ploughing into a closed screen door is normal. If you don't believe me, then next time you're at a friend's place, notice all the little rips and dents in *her* screen door and ask how it happened. Your friend will avert her eyes and say it was the cat. But cats don't smash through screens unless they're tanked, and most cats don't get enough allowance for that, which is good because cats don't know how to spend responsibly.

No matter how your metal-framed screen got holey, replacing it is easy. Yet there is towering potential for frustration. For one thing, screen doors are flimsy once you've taken them off their rigid tracks, so they twist, turn, and wobble around. If you're feeling short-tempered or hormonal, it's probably less stressful just to sell your house and start over in a home with its screens intact. Or you can try my screen-defeating tactics.

Tools

Screwdriver, framing square, drill, pliers, vacuum or whisk, spline roller, utility knife

Materials

Blocks, screws, screening, spline

Step 2: Loosening the adjustment screw.

Steps

1. Put on your lucky shorts and call for beer. The repair has begun.

2. Lift the bottom corner of the door a little so you can see a spring-mounted plastic wheel sitting astride a narrow aluminum track. Wedge the blade of a screwdriver underneath the wheel. Lift it up a little so the wheel retracts, and then pull the bottom edge of the screen door toward you a bit, so the wheel is no longer on its rail. If the wheel won't easily pop over the rail, loosen it by backing off its adjustment screw. The screw, usually a Phillips head, is located on the edge of the door near the wheel. Turn the screw counterclockwise a few turns and try again to pop the wheel over the rail.

3. Free the other bottom wheel the same way, and then swing the lower edge of the screen door out. With the timely help of gravity, the door will now drop out of the top groove, and you can carry it away to begin the meaty part of our procedure.

4. Lay the screen door on a horizontal work surface. Pause. This is the moment when you must choose between two forks in the road of life. One leads to annoyance, the other to profound aggravation. If you do not take immediate measures to prevent your door from skating around as you work, you will shorten your lifespan.

5. Use a framing square to make sure the door is lying square. Fasten the door in place by using a drill to screw down supporting blocks of wood butted up against the edges of the frame. (If you want to, screw right through the old screen into the inside blocks, because the screen is toast anyway, so why not add another hole?) Using blocks keeps all four sides of the door in position and holds it square so you don't end up with a freshly screened parallelogram that won't fit back into any door frame, ever. Don't ask me how I know this.

Step 5: Squaring, blocking, and securing the screen for surgery.

6. If you look carefully, you'll notice that the old screening is held in place on the frame by a length of "spline," thin flexible tubing that runs along a channel on the perimeter of the door. To remove the old spline, find a loose end and yank the whole length out with pliers. You'll probably have to remove some of the latch hardware at this point. I usually lose the screws, so I've found that taping them to my forehead saves time later.

7. Pull off the old holey screen. The channel is probably full of crud, so tidy it up. Nobody likes a dirty channel. If you don't have a vacuum handy, a whisk works.

8. Lay fresh screening over the door. Make sure you've bought screening material that is at least one inch wider than the door you're repairing. I bought stuff that was too narrow and the ensuing anguish was worse than wearing pantyhose backwards.

9. Screening is available by the yard or in rolls and comes in nylon, aluminum, fiberglass, and various other materials. Nylon is the easiest to work with. You'll also need a length of spline long enough to fill the channel and a spline roller, which looks like a pizza cutter. Spline rollers are inexpensive and generally poorly manufactured, but they do the job. Alternatively, you can push the spline into place with the tip of a screwdriver, although it won't provide the romance of using a spline roller. When pushing the spline into the channel, be careful not to stretch the splining material. The best way to install it is to seat the first inch of spline. Then, without stretching the splining cord, move your spline roller about four inches ahead and tuck the spline into the channel. Then run your spline roller backwards along the channel, tucking the spline into position.

   This ensures that you won't stretch the spline material during installation. Stretched spline cord eventually retracts and can leave you with gaps. Repeat the tuck-and-backwards-roll until you have seated the spline all the way around the outside of the door.

10. Trim off the excess screening with a utility knife. Reinstall the door by inserting the top wheels first and then swinging the bottom into place and lifting the wheels up and over the rail. Adjust the screws so the door is sitting square and riding the rails saucily once again.

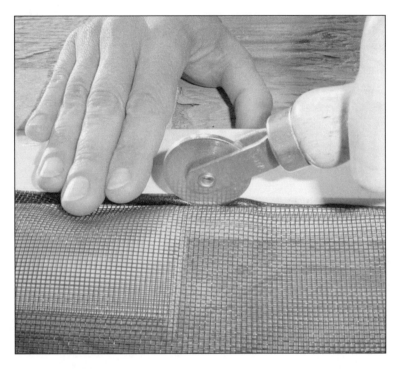

Step 9: Tucking the spline into place with a spline roller.

The beauty of this repair is that from now on, you won't need to remember that the screen door is there when you're hurrying outside with an armload of beverages, because you know how to fix a busted screen. There can be no greater confidence in this life.

3 UPGRADES

If you're optimistic when you start a project, you're setting yourself up for trouble. That's because you have not computed the statistical probability for failure. You think it is likely to go smoothly. Where you got this idea from is your imagination, because experience shows that no home upgrade has ever gone smoothly in the past. But for mysterious reasons, you are an optimist.

If by some miracle you could change this about yourself, you would have the option of being either a realist or a pessimist. Realists would not attempt the upgrade in the first place, because they would know that somebody would just come along and say, "I thought you were more realistic than to think you could accomplish something like that," and that kind of comment really gets realists' goat, if they actually had a goat, which they will be quick to point out they don't. The glory of being a pessimist is that no matter how badly the project goes, it'll turn out better than you had expected. Compared to optimists, pessimists at least have a chance of being pleasantly surprised.

Other People's Expectations

If you're going to try to improve anything in life, you're going to face criticism from others. Some forms of criticism are always difficult, like when somebody says, "How many beers did you have before you hung that shelf?" This is the kind of criticism that really smarts, because in your heart, you know it wasn't the beer that made the shelf crooked. Because you didn't have any beer.

So those critical comments cut deep and require an immediate retort. Something that implicates the critical party, if possible. Something like, "As many beers as you had the night we got married."

You have now started a dialogue, which, experts tell us, is the path to true understanding. Experts also tell us that criticism has to be delivered constructively. So when he says, "You should've tuned up the level before you attached that shelf," you can say, "I thought you tuned up the level that day you dropped it off the roof four times and kept calling me on your cell phone to come out and pass it back up to you."

Now you're really getting somewhere in supporting your partner's efforts at home repair. And experts say that's the kind of repeated generosity it takes to sustain a good marriage.

Hanky Planky

Plank flooring for any budget

As I approach the cusp of middle age, the closest I've come to having any design allegiance is that my furniture is the same stuff I had in college, which places me in the Early Student School of Decor. The one exception is the bedroom, where I have a high-end mattress, but only because my futon got so compacted, it was about to become the next black hole. *Bottom line:* You probably shouldn't take my decorating advice — unless you have the problem I'm about to describe, or you have hardwood tastes on a paint budget.

Here's the situation: I ripped out my old, musty carpeting to reveal a plywood subfloor, the perfect base for laying a hardwood floor or even installing reclaimed plank flooring, available from salvage supply places. Unfortunately, it's going to cost thousands of dollars for either hardwood or the reclaimed planks, even if I install it myself. Plus I can't decide which wood to choose, and anyway, delivery takes five to seven weeks. So I think, why make an expensive mistake now when I can make a much more expensive one in years to come, after lumber prices have gone sky-high? Why not just blunder cheaply now and save the really high-cost errors for later in life when I'm cresting the richly emotional foothills of perimenopause?

That decided, I covered the entire floor with a fantastic floor leveller product called DAP Concrete Patcher and Resurfacer (Dry Mix), a cement-based product that you trowel on. Happily, it has an extremely low shrinkage rate so you need only one coat, plus it's somewhat flexible when cured, so it won't crumble if your floor is a bit spongy. This

One of the most reliable ways to get design ideas is by drinking beer. But you have to be careful in mixed company because the ideas you get from beer can get you in trouble. Ideas like "I'll bet that guy thinks I'm pretty attractive," or "Yeah, that guy really digs me," or "Hey, that guy is drinking the same kind of beer as me; he must really be my type." Eventually, when the beer wears off you realize, "Yikes, that guy is my husband." That's a real shocker.

product is paintable after an hour or two. The only trick is that you have exactly ten minutes' working time after you've mixed the stuff. If you're not an Olympic-class troweler, mix small batches and don't pause for snacks. I mixed a huge batch and it set rock-hard in the bucket before I'd used a quarter of it, so now I have a giant, pail-shaped plug as a souvenir of my modest troweling skills.

Applying DAP Concrete Patcher and Resurfacer (Dry Mix).

After the concrete patcher has started to harden (about twenty minutes), scrape off any bumps or ridges. When it's completely dry, prime the surface with a good acrylic primer. This step will save chipping problems later. Then choose an appropriate color of porch and floor paint for the topcoat. (Porch and floor paint is a formulation that's long-wearing. Most manufacturers include porch and floor paint in their lines.) By way of honesty, it took me five topcoats because I kept selecting (oxymoron alert) "playful neutrals" and then had to cover them with another shade, which would turn out to be more ghastly than the last. After a pathetic parade of disappointments I marched to the paint counter and confessed to having no design sense. The nice lady pretended she didn't feel sorry for me and picked a fine color. *Moral*: Always get a second opinion if your paint has a name like Inner Fear or Rinsed Buffalo. Oh wait, they all have names like that. Get help.

Just before the final coat of paint, carve floorboard "cracks" using a Dremel (or an electric drill if you don't have a Dremel) fitted with a stone grinding wheel. Start by measuring and marking plank lines on the floor using a longish 2" × 4" board for a ruler. You can create random or regular board widths. I did seven-inch-wide planks but occasionally threw in a four-inch or ten-inch spacing to incorporate existing plywood seams, which look goofy if you let them fall in the middle of a "plank."

> **SAFETY ALERT!**
>
> • Dremels throw a lot of dust and are quite loud, so you'll need to wear safety glasses, a dust mask, and ear gear.

The edge of a grinding wheel makes a convincing V-groove.

Wearing safety glasses, ear gear, and a dust mask, cut V-grooves along the lines with your grinding bit. Vary the depth between ⅟₃₂ inch and ⅛ inch to forge different degrees of settling and wear. Freehand the carving so the lines are mildly irregular and wobbly, which is how real painted planks look. (Using a Dremel will make you feel like a god. This was the most fun I'd had since I tried to get the cat to use a pen; you just don't appreciate how good life is until you've watched a hairball with a grossly inflated ego and no opposable thumb try to sign a check to the vet.)

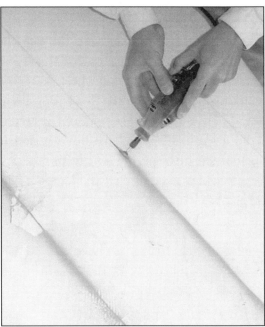

The Dremel rotary tool: your key to a new floor.   After priming, freehand the lines to mimic old planks.

Once you've finished carving, vacuum and give the floor a final topcoat. Depending on the color you (or the paint-counter lady) chose, you could rub a contrasting shade — say Incandescent Filth — into the lines to emphasize them, but it's not really necessary. If your floor is in a high-traffic area, cover the whole surface with a couple of coats of water-based urethane for a long-lasting finish.

This floor treatment satisfies tight schedules and taut purse strings, plus it really fools the senses. Here's proof. My brother-in-law Bill, who's a specialist in restoring antique houses, absolutely couldn't tell the floor was plywood. He was completely convinced we had a real painted pine surface. I guaranteed him it was just plywood, but I was dead smug about it. Total cost of doing one large room, including DAP Concrete Patcher and Resurfacer (Dry Mix) and paint: under $100. Sweet.

Faux on the Floor

Create a realistic-looking rug

Once you've coaxed a homely plywood subfloor into looking like well-aged painted planks, you're ready for a total artistic debauchery. How about adding a painted-on rug to top off your planks? The correct terminology for this optical illusion is *trompe l'oeil*, which is French for "fool the eye," a relative of faux. (*Faux* used to be a French word but was annexed by the English language during the late twentieth-century rash of home decor shows that were touted as reality-based, only all their techniques were faux-based. There's a brain crasher.)

Mo' Faux
The faux rug effect is fun to do and only takes a couple of afternoons. I used a sort of neo-Persian, semi-Celtic, Dr. Seuss-ish design that sprung unbidden from my twisted mind. (You can use stencils if you actually want your rug to look good.)

Ralph Waldo Emerson said, "There are no days in life so memorable as those which vibrate to some stroke of the imagination." When you're engrossed in a challenging project, this can be so true. Then again, so are the words of King George V, who said, "Always go to the bathroom while you have a chance."

TIPS

• Detail is critical. If you look at real Persian rugs or Celtic designs, you'll see that they're just drenched with insane detail. Add lots of tones and shades and build the three-dimensional quality of the rug bit by bit. If you're not graphically inclined, simple S and C shapes strung together can give you some great curlicue effects.

Faux the very first time.

Tools
Measuring tape, rags, stencils (optional), paintbrush, artist's palette knife, artist's brushes

Materials
Blue masking tape (won't pull up existing paint), pencil, spackle, lots of shades of decorator's acrylics (available in small, inexpensive bottles), water-based urethane

Steps

1. Sketch your design first on paper. *Warning:* You will probably not fully appreciate the importance of this step until
you're on your hands and knees painting *over* your first
attempt after a misguided crack at winging it. Yet another
lesson I learned in my usual manner: the hard way.

2. Measure and mark the outline of your rug on the floor
using blue masking tape, or just freehand it with a pencil
if you're in a hotdogging mood.

3. Paint the body of your rug on the floor using a base coat of
the rug's main color. Let it dry.

4. If you're painting over faux planks, you'll need to apply
spackle to the plank lines that fall within the rug's perimeter
or the finished rug will not fool the eye, or even fool the you.
An artist's palette knife works well for feathering spackle into
the delicate lines, as opposed to a big honking putty knife,
which is awkward to work with.

5. To get a soft, fibrous, carpetlike effect, dab on some spackle
mixed with a slightly darker shade of the base color (ratio is
about 50 percent spackle, 50 percent paint). Adding the
spackle will take all the gloss out of the paint by giving it just
enough texture to create millions of mini-shadows. Dab the
mixture evenly over the base color with a big brush to give
your rug a very matte, tufty-looking surface.

6. Once the surface is dry, use a measuring tape and pencil to
sketch out the basic design of your rug.

7. Start painting the design using a narrow, tough-bristled
artist's brush to dab rather than stroke the paint on. Use
a fairly dry brush so you get the look of fibers, not drippy
paint. If your acrylic paint is really glossy, add a little spackle
to tone it down.

8. Add tassels at each end of the rug. Tassels are the key
element that "sells" the rug as being a three-dimensional
object. Paint the tassels in a raggedy, helter-skelter way,

as though they are a tripping hazard, and then add shadows that coordinate with the main light source in the room.

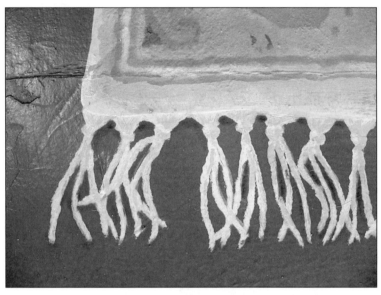

Shadowing the edge and the tassels makes the rug seem three-dimensional.

9. Paint the whole surface with several coats of clear, satin-finish, water-based urethane.

Invite friends over to see your luminous work of art. When people exclaim, "You faux, girl!" treat them to a winsome blush. But no matter how many accolades you receive from friends, there's no greater compliment to your faux skills than your cat sitting smack in the middle of the rug looking perplexed.

Sour Drapes

Hints on installing curtains

There are two kinds of people in the world: those who use towels and old blankets for curtains, and those who go to the trouble of installing proper drapes. Up until now, I've always been a towel girl. Tacking up towels is my way of being optimistic about moving to a better place soon. But at last I've landed in a house I like well enough to fix up with real curtains. This is the equivalent of landing a man and then correcting him whenever he's wrong about directions or grammar or women: You are finally investing in a stock you'll never want to trade up on, so it's worth the effort. (He will be flattered by your attention to his mistakes, knowing that your incessant corrections reflect your commitment to the relationship.)

Coincidentally, the curtain industry is as old as the institution of marriage, ostensibly because what people do after they're married requires curtains by law. Curtains have come a long way since they were a greasy animal hide tied across a cave entrance. For one thing, they can be staggeringly expensive compared to, say, a greasy animal hide. Also, they're now called "window treatments" by those in the know, although you still won't catch most people saying, "I feel frisky. Let's close the window treatments."

If you paid handsomely for your window coverings, or even if you didn't but you still want them to look great, here are some installation hints from a reformed towel devotee:

1. Think about your window for a moment. Builders don't just cut a hole in a building and call it a window. They

As Aristotle said, "All art is concerned with coming into being." So it doesn't matter how "artistic" your curtain installation looks, because you defined yourself in the doing. Keep this up and you'll eventually be able to look yourself up in the dictionary.

TIPS

• When selecting a bit to use in predrilling a hole for a hollow-wall anchor, test the anchor itself in the empty hole in the drill index to see if the hole is a good snug fit for the tubular anchor. There's nothing like the disappointment of an oversized hole.

• When you're mounting window hardware you need to be in a finicky mood, with the kind of anal, exacting, pinched concentration you had the last time you decided to alphabetize your freezer contents. Believe it or not, there is a use for that state of mind. The best thing is that once you get your curtains hung, you'll feel so perky that you might need to close them right away.

have to reinforce the edges of the opening so the rest of the wall doesn't collapse into the space. To that end, they put a stout miniature beam in place across the top edge of the window. This "header" carries the load of the building across the span of the window opening. Technically, you're supposed to screw into this header when you're mounting curtain hardware, because merely screwing into drywall may not offer enough support for the weight of the fabric and/or hardware. But screwing into wood isn't always practical. (See #2.)

2. Your window may have wide trim, and the header may not extend beyond the trim. It would look strange to mount curtain-rod brackets through the trim into the header. So you can try to find a stud, but you probably won't find one in the very perfect spot you've chosen to mount your bracket. In this case you *must* use hollow-wall anchors to keep the screws from chewing up the drywall and then falling out, taking your drapes with them. If you have lath and plaster walls, toggle bolt anchors work best. (You can tell if you have lath and plaster walls by trying to push a thumbtack into the wall. If it doesn't penetrate no matter how hard you push, you have a plaster surface.)

3. Traditionally, window height is set to match door height in a room. Check your room for this truism. If your windows are set lower than the door height, your curtains may appear heavy and oppressive. Try raising the level of the curtain rod to the height of the doors to provide a feeling of balance and expansiveness. Also, the higher you set your curtain rod, the farther you can extend its width on either side of the window trim without the proportions looking dorky.

4. To position your mounting brackets, run an imaginary forty-five-degree line off the corner of the existing trim. Most trim is mitered, so just extend the line of the miter

joint and place your bracket somewhere on that line according to what feels right to your eye. Copy the position of that bracket at the opposite corner of the window, then drill and mount the hardware.

SAFETY ALERT!

• When you're drilling at eye level, it's especially important to wear those safety glasses.

Step 4: Setting the brackets in line with the miter joint.

5. There are a zillion configurations of mounting hardware. Read the manufacturer's directions once and then follow your own instincts. *One warning:* If the instructions say to use a level to establish the rod's horizontal position, *ignore* this advice. Most walls are not perfectly plumb and most windows and ceilings are not perfectly level. If you religiously set the rod using a level, then the window trim may look crooked, or the ceiling may appear wacky, probably because it is. To avoid the misfortune of a crooked rod, it's critical to align it with either the trim or the ceiling, whichever is closest to the plane of your rod.

If You Can't Take the Seat, Get Outta the Bathroom

Upgrading a toilet seat

The great inventor Thomas Edison said, "If we all did the things we are capable of doing, we would literally astound ourselves." For me, that would mean walking through a room without bumping into things. I can dream.

You can upgrade your bathroom decor by trading up your toilet seat. The job has bleak moments. This is because you end up lying under a toilet, which takes you back to the first time you got drunk. This briefly reminds you that you still have everything that you had then, except now it's all lower. But don't dwell on these things like I'm doing now. Instead, go to the hardware store and choose a shiny new toilet seat.

Tools
Safety goggles, gloves, wrench or pliers, mini-hacksaw (optional)

Materials
Pillow (optional), penetrating oil, new toilet seat (washers and nuts are included), duct tape (optional), Vaseline

Fun Quotient
Better than getting your bum caught in a cracked seat

Steps
1. When you get home from the hardware store, lie down under the toilet. A pillow will enhance your comfort; you're going to be here awhile.
2. Wear goggles to protect yourself from flying "matter," a nice word for the stuff that collects around the bolts that hold the old toilet seat in place.

3. Your first job is to get the nuts off. It is seldom a matter of simply removing the nuts. This is because the nuts are corroded with rust and "matter." How did it get there? Mysterious aiming problems of other family members is a safe bet. This is certainly the time to own a good pair of gloves you can throw out at the end of the job. Or, if you decry wastefulness and you happen to know someone in the nuclear industry, you can get the gloves radiated for future use on other jobs.

TIPS

• When you need to take a quick measurement in a hardware store but you've forgotten to bring a measuring tape, don't fret. Use your body parts for a new and interesting purpose. One day when you have some extra time and a measuring tape, find out how wide your hand span is. The adult hand span doesn't change much over the course of a lifetime, so it's a consistent measurement to know and use. Mine is exactly eight inches, so I can never be fooled.
(continued on p. 106)

Step 8: Tightening the nuts on the new seat.

TIPS

(continued from p.105) It's also useful to know the length of other body parts, like the top phalange of your thumb, the middle phalange of your baby finger, the bottom phalange of your middle finger (the finger used in traffic), and the distance between your elbow and the tip of your baby finger. Have fun with your body parts, and other people's too if you're not shopping alone.

4. Speaking of jobs, it's a good idea to post a sign on the bathroom door directing others to take their business to alternate facilities while you are working.

5. Start by loosening the nuts under the rim of the bowl with a wrench or pliers. If they're corroded and won't turn, apply penetrating oil to the threads and wait five minutes for it to soak in.

6. If the nuts still won't turn, saw through the bolts with a mini-hacksaw, being careful not to scratch the porcelain surface of the toilet. Protect it with duct tape if necessary.

7. Once you have the nuts off, lift off the old seat. Save it if you like, and later you can turn it into a mirror-bottomed serving tray. Talk about a great conversation starter.

8. Install the new seat with the washers and nuts provided. Most modern seats have plastic or brass nuts and bolts to prevent rusting. If they're metal, rub Vaseline into the threads before tightening the nuts; this will make your next seat upgrade easy. No matter what your nuts are made of, never overtighten them. You can actually crack the porcelain of the toilet.

Mud, Sweat, and Cheers

Classy wall veneers that anyone can do

One thing I've always liked about being human is that when you have a problem, you can pretty much guarantee you're not alone. One of the billions of other people on this planet has already had your problem and figured out a way to solve it. All you need to do is find that person and ask her how she did it. That person could be right next to you on the bus, or down the hall at the office. That's why it's important to complain about your problem to everyone you see, all day long. This increases your chances of finding the solution to your problem, while simultaneously reducing the number of people who want to sit near you, so you'll always have plenty of legroom.

As a case in point, I had a pesky problem in my basement. Drywall had been installed on one wall, but it had not been taped and mudded. Now, there must be at least one other person whose garage, cabin, or basement walls have been drywalled in that wacky "Shabby Shirk" style by a contractor who worked on it for one morning and then had a better idea and headed for the local bar.

When we first moved in, I painted our unfinished wall. I knew I was just putting off the unavoidable, but I had reasons. Taping and mudding drywall is a tedious process. It takes a huge effort to get the wall really smooth. The prospect of mixing up a batch of drywall compound, applying, fussing, feathering, cleaning equipment, washing clothing, scrubbing self, waiting for the mud to dry, scraping, sanding, remixing, reapplying, letting dry again, sanding, vacuuming, repeating, and finally painting is — call me lazy — a bit daunting. No wonder that contractor went out drinking.

If you've got unfinished or hacked-up walls somewhere in your home, cabin, or garage, or walls that are wildly uneven or full of dings and scrapes, you need a quick solution that covers easily, won't cost a mint, and doesn't require hiring anyone. So here's what I did. This technique doesn't demand patience or experience. It's cheap, fun, and easy, plus I didn't even have to paint afterwards.

First, I bought a big tub of drywall compound. I mixed some latex paint into the drywall compound until I had a creamy (but not runny) texture that was color-coordinated

The biggest benefit of working with your hands is that you get a little grin on your face because you feel content. People make assumptions about what that grin means and deduce that your life is much more fascinating than it actually is. Why ruin it for them?

TIPS

• If your textured walls are in a high-traffic, spatter-prone area, wait until the finish is completely cured and then give it a coat or two of water-based urethane. That'll make it washable.

with the rest of the room. You can also mix earth pigment powders or tinting concentrates into the compound if you want more intense colors.

The heavy texture helps to disguise wall flaws.

I started slapping the tinted compound onto the walls using a six-inch drywall knife. I scooped the compound onto my knife and gobbed it onto the wall surface as fast as I could, making lots of random passes and "knocking down" the high spots, dragging the trowel in various directions and letting it skip over the surface so the final effect was textural and highly bodacious.

After the compound had set for a couple of hours and was starting to get hard, I went over it with a damp rag, smoothing and softening it. This created a velvety finish that covers the fact that the drywall joints weren't flush.

Fun with Mud

You can accomplish lots of spirited finishes with drywall mud. Try dragging a whisk or broom through the freshly applied compound, or swirling it with a damp sponge. For a classic California finish (I call it California because I've only seen this wall texture there), dab compound onto the wall using a stiff-bristled stucco brush, and then flatten the high points with a big drywall knife for a kind of squashed-blob effect.

Once it is partially dry, the surface can be made as smooth as you like with a damp rag or sponge.

If, at the start of your venture, you added tint or latex paint to the compound, the finish is now done. If you don't like the color you got, you can just paint over it or apply a glaze.

Humble drywall mud gives you a chance to play with different kinds of strokes and patterns. It's an utterly romantic and forgiving medium. You can also mix different shades of tinted mud and layer them to achieve a three-dimensional effect. Or squeeze some metallic paint into the mud for a nightclub finish.

The great advantages of these "skip-trowel" and "knock-down" techniques are that they're economical, good-looking, uncomplicated, and fast. Plus they hide all kinds of imperfections. The final effect of this organic-looking finish will make you feel like a princess, unless you're a guy, in which case you're no doubt still fairly pleased with yourself.

Is that fun or what? I'm betting I don't need to sit beside you on the bus to know how you're going to solve your pesky wall problems this weekend.

Bug of War!

Defeat fashion-eating insects naturally

When you're young you can make people think you're competent just by wearing the right outfit, but I've made enough mistakes by now that I can't fool people anymore.

Sometimes though, one still has to make the effort. Like when the in-laws are coming for a visit. I've only met my in-laws once in thirteen years, right after the elopement, and the impression I made probably wasn't favorable. Now they're coming to see us, so I'll have a chance to appear respectable in a conservative suit. Only trouble is, my suit has tiny chunks missing. Chunks the size of a moth's mouth. So now I'm hypersensitive about moths, silverfish, and other tiny munching heathen.

Here's a solution based on what people do in the Deep South, where moths are the size of oxen. The Southern secret is to line closets with aromatic cedar. Bugs hate the smell and move on to someone else's closets. Aromatic cedar is sold in hardware stores in two formats: mixed lengths or forty-eight-inch lengths. I went with the uniform forty-eight-inch boards and installed them vertically, like wainscoting, instead of horizontally, like the inside of a sauna. *Note:* Aromatic cedar shavings are what we Canadians use to line hamster cages, so you may be put off when your clothes smell like rodent bedding. Get past that psychological barrier and you're moth-free. *Other note:* You can do this the fast way, meaning you just slap the cedar up and call it done, or you can do it the classy way, which means removing the baseboard and then replacing it once the cedar is installed. I'm assuming you want a high-end job (to match your suit), so here goes:

If you're ever whittling and someone says, "Hey, what're you making?" it's good to laugh so hard they get mad and walk away. Because you don't know what you're making. Your mind is just wandering and the stick is there to make you look productive. If they press you for an answer, say you're creating a realistic carving of a stick.

Tools
Utility knife, pry bars, tongue-and-groove pliers, pencil, stud finder, hammer, measuring tape, straightedge, safety glasses, ear protection, handsaw or power miter saw, nail set, drill (optional)

Materials
Boric acid powder (optional), aromatic cedar, Loctite Power Grab adhesive, finish nails, wood putty or paintable caulk, cap rail, primer and paint

Eleven Steps to Bugless Smugness
1. Remove clothing (not *that* clothing — the stuff in the closet) and any existing shelving.
2. Using a utility knife, cut through caulking along the top of the baseboard and in the mitered corners. Pull back any carpeting. Start removing baseboard next to the doorway where

TIPS

• Install the cedar boards as soon as you open the box! Cedar is famous for twisting and bowing in response to humidity and temperature changes.

• If you're adding nails to keep boards straight, don't nail too close to the tongue-edge of the board. You'll just have trouble fitting the next groove over the tongue because the installed board is set too tight against the wall.

there's a square cut end. Use pry bars to gently lift the baseboard away from the wall. Don't force it aggressively; you'll just split it and have to replace it, and if your home is older, good luck matching what you busted.

3. Tidy up the baseboard pieces, removing old caulk with a utility knife. Pull nails out by yanking them through from the bad side using tongue-and-groove pliers. Don't split the dang baseboard!

4. If you have really intense bug issues, sprinkle boric acid powder (a great natural bug repellent that's about as toxic as table salt) around the edge of the closet prior to installing the cedar.

5. Mark a top horizontal edge so you know how far up to go. All my boards were forty-eight inches tall, but you might be working with mixed lengths, so decide accordingly. Use a stud finder to mark the stud locations so you have the option of nailing into studs.

Step 6: A squiggle or two of Loctite Power Grab does the trick.

6. Start installing boards next to the trim inside the door of the closet. Put several squiggles of adhesive on the rough side of the first board. Use latex-based Loctite Power Grab adhesive instead of traditional panel glue or construction adhesive. Power Grab has a built-in trigger, so you don't need a caulking gun. It adheres really fast, cleans up with soapy water, and has no odor. Once you've applied adhesive to the back of the board, place the board's grooved edge against the door trim and press into position.

7. If a board is curvy, bowed, or twisted and won't line up properly, nail the board in place with finish nails in addition to the adhesive. Nail into studs where possible, but leave the nail heads sticking up about an eighth of an inch, then sink them later with a nail set. By the way, if you have an older house you probably have lath and plaster walls, so predrill for the nails or you'll just bend 'em on the unyielding plaster beneath.

8. Periodically measure the distance from the top and bottom of your ongoing installation to the next corner, so you know if the boards are plumb relative to the upcoming corner. If things are off-kilter, cheat by subtly tilting the next few boards. When you reach the corner, you'll probably have to rip a board down to fit the remaining space. If the space isn't square, measure the top and bottom dimensions of the space and mark a fresh board accordingly. Use a straightedge to connect the two marks, and then cut along the line. If your cut is inaccurate or really gnarly, you can always run cove molding vertically in all the corners to cover unsightly gaps or rough edges.

9. Once you've installed all the cedar, use a handsaw or power miter saw to trim your baseboard pieces to fit the new dimensions of your closet (since you've added ⅜ inch of cedar on all sides, the baseboard won't fit any more). If you're using a power saw, don't forget to wear your ear and eye protection.

Step 8: Measuring the distance to the next corner so the boards match the same degree of plumbness.

10. Reinstall the baseboard using fresh finish nails. If you have carpeting in your closet, reinstall your baseboard a half-inch up from the floor surface, giving your carpet room to run underneath the baseboard. If you have hardwood floors, reinstall the baseboard flush against the flooring. Sink the nail heads with a nail set. Fill nail holes with wood-filler putty or caulking, and touch up with paint if necessary.

11. Recaulk the corners of the baseboard; don't bother caulking along the top of the baseboard — it looks messy on the grooved cedar.

12. Add optional cap rail (sometimes called ply cap) to trim out the top edge of the cedar. Cap rail is notched at the back to fit over wainscoting or paneling. Prime and paint the cap rail *before* installation — it's way easier. Install the cap rail with Power Grab and an occasional finish nail. You'll probably have to caulk heavily along the top edge of the cap rail, since the cedar is thicker than what cap rail is designed to cover.

The end of munching moths.

That's it. Lining your closets with cedar adds huge value to your home and protects your fashion investments. Then when your visiting in-laws say, "Do I smell hamster?" smile smugly and say, "We're having it for dinner." That'll impress them even if your suit doesn't.

Extreme Shelf-Interest

Limitless custom shelving

Here's a multiple-choice question for people who live in buildings of any kind:

Which single item would set off the biggest cherry bomb of delight for you?
1. Cosmetic surgery
2. A weekend in Majorca
3. A $10,000 spending spree at the mall

Euclidean geometry has produced more sweat on the palms of math students than even the raging flush of adolescent attraction. What history doesn't tell us about Euclid is that he was probably tough to cook for. For example, who can produce a perfectly circular pancake? I think we can all hypothesize that Euclid's domestic partner was probably pretty testy.

4. Regular bowels

5. Extra shelving

Most people would pick #5. In terms of basic human drives, "having enough shelves" falls between food and sex. Shelves, however, usually provide the most consistent satisfaction. Hence, knowing how to install your own shelves is the key to well-being. Here's proof: When I was in my twenties I shared living quarters with two other people. We had a tiny kitchen that possessed only two cupboards, into which we crammed our glasses and dishes. This left us with nowhere to put food or cooking equipment, so we stacked it high on the teeny kitchen counter. But then we had no surface area for cutting up vegetables or fruit, so we were forced to live on popcorn.

Finally one of my housemates — let's call him Don — measured a closet, drove to the hardware store, bought planks, came home, banged around a bit, and suddenly we had six glorious shelves to hold all our tins, cookware, snack foods, and beer. That day was the highlight of my twenties. It was the day I realized that shelf-knowledge is power.

I want to share that power with you. So here's Don's number . . . No! What am I saying? One must discover shelf-knowledge for oneself. Here's the easiest way of achieving shelf-realization in your own closet. You don't have to fuss with kits or awkward, bulky brackets. This design is simple, elegant, easy, and, if you use cedar, repels bugs and imparts a great fragrance to linens.

Tools

Electronic stud finder, measuring tape, level, pencil, safety glasses, ear protection, saw, sander, drill

Materials

1" × 6" cedar boards, Loctite Power Grab adhesive, 3" screws (for attaching ledgers to studs), 1⅝" screws (for attaching shelves to ledgers)

TIPS

• Design tip: If you can operate a router, put a decorative edge on the front board of each shelf.
• Droopy tip: If your shelves are quite wide and they sag in the middle, add a triangular shelf support in the center of the span, screwing it to the wall and to the underside of the shelf.

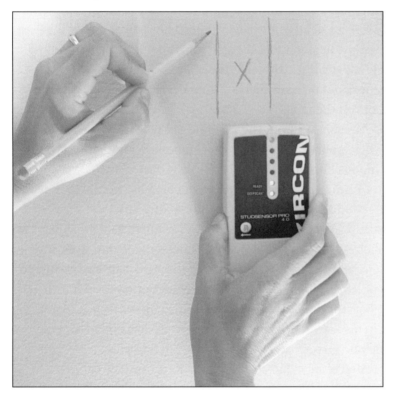

Either find the studs and nail into them or just use Loctite Power Grab and glue the ledgers to the wall.

Steps

1. Mark stud locations on the closet walls using an electronic stud finder (pocket model available for about $15 — a must-have for every human over the age of twelve). If any of the closet walls are riddled with plumbing, electrical conduit, heating ducts, or phone outlets, don't bother marking the studs. You won't be screwing into that wall because you could hit something important. Instead, use Loctite Power Grab glue — half the trouble, twice the fun.

2. Mark the appropriate height for the bottom shelf on the wall. *Hint:* Allow enough room for existing boxes or bins to rest on the floor underneath that first shelf.

3. Use a level to draw a continuous horizontal line at the marked height along the side walls and back wall of the closet; you'll use this reference line to locate the "ledger," a horizontal board that will support the back edge of your bottom shelf.

4. Measure up from the first line to the level of the ledger that will support your second shelf, and make another level, continuous horizontal line.

5. Continue measuring up and drawing horizontal ledger lines until you have reached the top of your closet.

6. Rip ledgers out of the same wood you're using for the shelves. The ledgers should be roughly 1½ inches wide and long enough to run the width of the shelf. The easiest way to cut ledger boards is to use a tablesaw, but not everyone has a big fancy tablesaw. I used a cutting guide attached to my circular saw to make a nice even cut. Using a handsaw would be raw torture, so try to avoid that heartbreak.

7. Attach the ledgers to stud locations using three-inch screws, or glue them to the wall using Loctite Power Grab adhesive (which is packaged in a really cool dispenser that gives you fantastic control over the amount of glue you use). Power Grab holds like a badger. You really don't even need to screw, but I always do anyway, owing to an over-enthusiastic nature.

8. Next, cut the shelf boards. I used four boards to make each twenty-two-inch-deep shelf. You may want to sand the boards, especially if you're planning to store linen on your new shelves. For foolproof cutting, measure the width of your closet at the front and back. The shelf boards will probably need to be cut in graduating sizes because most closets are not square! For example, if your closet is slightly wider at the front than at the back, but you cut all the boards the same length as the back board, you'll discover that the front boards are too short. Talk about irritating.

9. Dry-fit the shelf boards, and then predrill and screw them to the ledgers.

10. Load up shelves.

11. Gloat.

Basking in shelf-esteem.

Not Tonight, Dear, I've Got a Storage Issue

Mounting utility units

If you're not a geometrically precise person, you already know that simply guessing the center of something is as good as measuring for it. Just make sure you always live in an older dwelling with tilted floors and crooked walls, where anything hanging straight would completely ruin the mood.

Sometimes I dream that I live in a storage solutions catalog. All my shirts are white linen, hung in cavernous closets on identical wooden hangers spaced exactly two and a half inches apart. The surface of my desk is vacant but for tasteful accessories. My immaculate laundry room has a multiunit hamper with white canvas bags for every shade of dirt. My basement boasts rows of white storage cabinets, sparsely stocked by a rigidly minimalist designer.

When my eyes flutter open, the images of an orderly lifestyle pucker and retreat. I get up and pull on the gritty workclothes I left in a heap beside the bed. There's one answer to the frown on my face, and it's not Botox. It's storage space, and I aim to get some. I hop in the truck. The truck knows the route to the home improvement center without my help, so I just lean back and suck on an iced cappuccino.

The home improvement center is displaying a perky three-door cabinet, fully assembled. I'm starting to feel a spring in my step. I load the unit onto my truck, drive back to the house, and horse the cabinet into the basement. My pocket-model electronic stud finder goes to work identifying the edges of each stud behind the faux paneling. One of these mornings, that paneling has to go, but in the meantime, I've got a unit to mount.

I heave the new cabinet onto the laundry table. With the rear of the unit facing me, I center it on the wall. I trace the side edges of the cabinet onto the wall with chalk so I don't have to think about positioning details when I'm caught up in the white heat of the actual mounting procedure. I'm not in the mood for elaborate measuring, so I get creative. Improvising has gotten me into trouble in the past, but I've got a feeling my luck is about to change.

Using a square, I transfer the stud locations from the wall onto the mounting strips that run along the back of the cabinet. I drill pilot holes through both top and bottom mounting strips at the exact stud locations. I set the cabinet aside. This is going well. Perhaps too well. I hang a temporary 2" × 4" ledger on the wall to support the weight of the cabinet while I'm busy screwing it in place. Experience reminds me that if the ledger isn't installed on the level, the cabinet won't be either, so I use the longest level I own to ensure this ledger is dead horizontal. I predrill and screw the ledger into two of the studs. I'm building an appetite, but nothing that beer and chips can't handle. Oh, wait. I'm using power tools. Better make that beer and pretzels. The last thing I need is a slippery tool coming between me and a precision mounting job.

I call for a relative to help lift the cabinet onto the ledger. The relative is listless and preoccupied. This forces me to remove the cabinet doors because I know they'll just swing open and hit one of us in the teeth. Overbites run in our family. So do fix-it accidents. Mostly because we work with our mouths open.

Next, I make a T-jig (a couple of pieces of 2" × 4" screwed together to form a T-shape) and trim it to match the height of the ledger. The relative and I lift the cabinet and rest it on the ledger, aligning the sides to match those chalky reference marks I made earlier. I insert the T-jig to hold the weight of the front edge of the cabinet. With my free hand I brace the top of the cabinet against the wall. The relative stares into space. I'm on my own here. I drive a screw confidently through one of the pilot holes I drilled earlier.

TIPS

• If you're installing your cabinet above an existing counter, don't use a level to set your ledger. Why? Because the floor your counter is sitting on may not be level, so your cabinet will look weird if it's perfectly level but the counter beneath it is slanted one way or another. Instead, measure up from the surface of the counter and match that plane.

A T-jig and temporary ledger take the weight off.

SAFETY ALERT!

I was just kidding about the beer.

Then it happens. The screw spins. I can't feel it bite into wood. I've missed the stud. I tell the relative to take a break. I need a moment alone. I retrace my steps. Then a slow grin covers my mug as I suddenly remember that the relative and I happened to rotate the cabinet end to end when we were lifting it into position. D'oh! So that's why the pilot holes aren't lining up with the studs.

There are four possible solutions to this conundrum. I toy with each of them:

1. Flip the cabinet end to end. (It's completely reversible.)

2. Shift the cabinet sideways a bit so the predrilled holes line up with the studs. (I can use the screws in the ledger for visual reference.)

3. Instead of shifting the cabinet, which happens to be perfectly centered where it is, I can start the drill bit in the original pilot hole, but angle the bit enough that it finds the stud location by traveling at a jaunty slant.

4. Simply redrill new holes adjacent to the botched ones, with the relative steadying the unit while I do the real work.

The first step on the long road to organization.

I go with option #3. I like the hotdogging intensity of drilling on an angle. Once I drive a couple of upper screws, the cabinet holds its own. I release the relative from duty and finish the screwing with a reduced sense of urgency. I'm almost done. I unscrew the temporary ledger, install the cabinet shelves and hardware, and load that baby up with laundry accessories.

I go to sleep and dream of storage units — not the ones in the catalog, but the ones in my basement. They may not make me flawlessly organized, but I'm less cranky, and where I come from, that means a lot.

4   PROJECTS

Sometimes I hear people say, "I couldn't do that; I'm not artistic." Well, putting pressure on yourself to be artistic sets the bar a notch higher than your own height, and if you've ever done any high jumping, you'll know that's an awkward crash waiting to happen. If instead you say, "Maybe I'll just fool around with this a bit," you can actually surprise yourself and even some skeptical relatives. The gods of creativity will reward you when you give yourself permission to be a goof. They also reward perseverance, so don't give up. After all, the phrase "knowing when to quit" was invented by people who couldn't sense the potential in a pail full of broken hinges.

And I don't know about you, but if I don't get regular opportunities to work with my hands, I get kind of antsy. Different body parts need their own specific outlets, and when it comes to being easily bored, hands are right up there with mouths. Either one of them can get you into trouble, sometimes both at once.

Leonardo da Vinci put it a little differently when he said, "Where the spirit does not work with the hands, there is no art." So when you're about to begin making something with your hands, it's probably good to tune in to your spirit first. I'm not sure how one goes about this, but a fine start is always chips and beer.

You can make amazing things with your hands, and what you make will be unique, because you are unique. Your medium doesn't have to be glamorous. Lately I've been sculpting plasticine. Michelangelo said, "I saw the angel in the marble and carved until I set him free." So far, I haven't seen any angels in the plasticine, only a kind of toad shape. But that gives me hope.

Undertaking an artistic project, no matter how minor, is satisfying but usually messy. This is because your mind is preoccupied with a bigger vision, so you don't really notice the stains, spills, and burnt hair. And that's a gift. (The ability to clean up is a gift too, and some of us just don't have that gift.)

Once you're working away, caught up in a lather of creativity, you're in a state of optimism. You only believe in the best possible outcome for your efforts. Whether this is a state of grace, or pure denial, is only obvious when the project is done.

The following projects are so fulfilling that you can end up in a spacey bubble of contentment. Aristotle said, "There was never a genius without a tincture of madness." This means that if you're feeling a bit loopy as you work, you could be showing signs of genius. Great artists are often noted for being eccentric. Of course, there are some people who think that the weirder they get, the more artistic they are. But I've tried this and it doesn't work. If you don't believe me, I'll show you my collection of berets.

Rock around the Cloth!

Easy, wild, and colorful furniture for kids

There are at least three brilliant and soul-satisfying reasons for rolling up your sleeves and plunging into this project:
1. You've been tempted to try woodworking but don't know where to begin.
2. Hot days and bored kids are giving you a puzzling rash.
3. You have a wild imagination that's gotten you into trouble before.

Anyone can build furniture. Children's furniture is a good place to start because you can learn the basics. And if you make any boo-boos you can tell the kids you did that on purpose to match their personalities.

I've never had children, but that wouldn't stop me from writing a book called *Childrearing Suggestions from People Without Children*, which would be a collection of entertaining stunts and practical jokes to get children ready for the real world.

Kidding around.

Tools
Measuring tape, pencil, jigsaw with scrolling blade, safety glasses, ear protection, drill and bits, clamps

Materials
4' × 4' sheet of ¾" plywood, glue, dozen 1½" screws, fabric, acrylic artist's medium

Dimension guidelines for my bench:
27" – height of sides
12" – height of seat, measured from the ground
11" – depth of seat
24" – approximate overall width of throne

Going Loopy
Start by measuring the intended sitter's lower leg length, from the floor to the crease behind the knee. This will give you the ideal seat height, plus a chance to see if your child is washing behind his or her knees.

Next, lazily sketch loopy design ideas on a small piece of paper. Try using square Post-it notes for your design sketches. They have a casual quality, so you won't get all tense about making a "good" design. After all, you're just doodling. Experiment with curvy, squiggly lines until you get a chair profile that looks whimsical and good-natured. This project is so intuitive and spontaneous that any shape will do. You can't go wrong even if you have your eyes shut. In fact, I recommend drawing a few lines with your eyes shut. That way if the finished project is disturbingly bad, you can say, "It's pretty good, considering I had my eyes shut."

Now transfer a full-size version of the sidepiece onto a 4' × 4' piece of ¾-inch plywood, making sure the seat height is accurately marked. Remember, the wackier the design, the more fun it'll be to decorate. Indulge your inner goof.

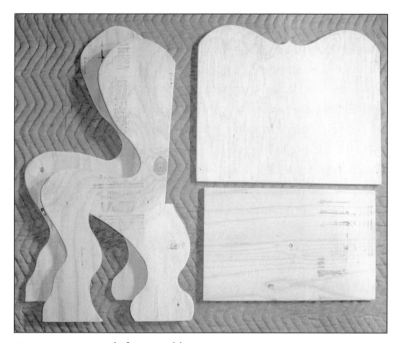

Cut-out pieces, ready for assembly.

Cut along the outline using a jigsaw fitted with a scrolling blade. Then use the piece you've just cut as a template to trace a mirror image for the other sidepiece. (Or make the second one asymmetrical if that's the mood you're in.) Next, cut out a rectangular bench seat, making sure the piece is wide enough to accommodate your little one's bottom. Then sketch an outline of the shape you want for the back of the bench, and cut it out.

Notch So Fast

After you've cut out the main pieces, try fitting them together. When you look at the chair from the side, the back piece is not in the same plane as the sides. To fix this, cut a ¾-inch notch down the back edge of each sidepiece (in a straight line from the top edge down to the level of the seat). Then the back will sit smartly in the notches and flush with the sides. Sweet.

TIPS

• Small fabric swatches (1½ square inches) can be ordered in batches of six hundred from Keepsake Quilting, 1-800-865-9458, www.keepsakequilting.com.

All you need now are some ledgers to hold the seat in position. I have an idea! Why not use those ¾-inch strips left over from cutting out the notches! Is this easy or what? Glue and screw one ledger in place on each sidepiece, measuring up from the bottom edges to make sure the ledgers are level.

For the final assembly, smear glue along all edges that come in contact with each other. Clamp the back and side pieces together with the seat in position. Predrill pilot holes and install 1½-inch screws into the seat through the back and sidepieces to provide extra support.

Fab, Oh!

To create an invincible upholstery-look finish, cut up a whole lot of fabric scraps. Separate the fabric pieces into color groups, sorting light and dark hues so you can graduate the tones and make it look like an airbrushed 1960s Volkswagen. Or do it some other way that will actually look good.

Apply the fabric pieces by brushing acrylic artist's medium (available at art supply stores in either gloss or matte finish) onto the plywood. Press a piece of fabric onto the brushed-on acrylic medium and then brush another coat over the top of the fabric. Repeat about six hundred times until your collage has spread over the whole surface.

If you like, trim each edge of the throne with a long ¾-inch strip of fabric. Once the whole thing is dry, you can apply a few coats of water-based urethane to make the "upholstery" indestructible.

This wildly unique furniture can be made to fit any bottom, so don't hold back. Your home is your castle, so make a few throne chairs for yourself too. And here's another idea: Cover all the walls of a room in the same kind of fabric patches as you put on your chairs, and then nobody will even be able to see your furniture. Who says op art is dead?

Finished throne.

Chest Do It

The easiest "hope" chest ever

If you're going to get lucky, you want to set the stage. So most of us are familiar with the hasty purchase of overpriced undergarments on the occasion of an anniversary, a big date, or the office Christmas party. In the old days, women didn't make impulsive underwear purchases. Starting at the dawn of adolescence they began embellishing knickers with come-hither embroidery, fashioning coy lace for camisoles, and festooning their drawers with pink rosettes. They were encouraged in their travails by overwrought maiden aunts whose own burgeoning hope chests were testaments to the diverted libido. I think it's ironic that the accepted method of curbing waywardness in young girls was the continuous plunging of a needle in and out of folds of cotton, but maybe that's just me.

For today's rambunctious woman, carpentry is way less restrained and — here's a bonus — infinitely louder.

Even if you're already married, it's not too late to build a hope chest. It's your way of saying, "Honey, of all the men I've loved, you're the one who's put up with me the longest, so go ahead, pick something racy out of the hope chest and if it still fits, I'll wear it." This will help generate hope for the immediate future, especially for your husband.

Tools
Measuring tape, saw, countersink bit, drill, clamps, knife, lighter or matches, hammer, sandpaper and/or electric sander

Materials
Lumber (see cut list), 1½" wood screws, 1" wood screws, about 3' of heavy nylon rope for handles, 30" piano hinge (cut a longer hinge to length using a hacksaw if you can't find a 30" precut hinge), ¾" brass screws to attach piano hinge, 12" piece of steel chain, fifty-eight ¼" hardwood plugs (or size that fits the countersink bit you're using), two ¾" steel

TIPS

• If you don't have a helper or prehensile pectorals, it helps to have several sets of Quick-Grip clamps to hold the pieces together when you're assembling. You can even get Quick-Grip corner clamps that hold two pieces at a ninety-degree angle. Sweet. Ask for clamps on all your birthdays.

screws to attach chain, food-grade beeswax polish for non-toxic finish

Cut list

Bottom: 1" × 6" cedar decking – 3 pieces, each 28½" long. Make sure the cedar you get is the typical milled dimension of 1" × 5½". Otherwise the rest of your cut list must be adjusted to fit the bottom dimension, because your bottom will be too big or too small. As if anyone's ever satisfied with his or her bottom.

Sides: 1" × 8" pine – 4 pieces, each 16½" long

Front and back: 1" × 8" pine – 4 pieces, each 30" long

Corner posts: 2" × 2" pine – 4 pieces, each 13½" long

Lid: 1" × 10" pine – 2 pieces, each 31" long (to overhang ½")

Lid strapping: 1" × 2" pine – 2 pieces, each 14" long

Bottoms Up

This chest is built using basic crate construction. The walls are held in place by four corner posts. First, lay out the bottom boards and measure across the width of your three boards to make sure it adds up to 16½ inches. If it doesn't, stop *before* you cut the rest of your lumber. You need side-pieces that match the exact width of the bottom, so account for this in the rest of your cuts!

End over End

Build one of the short ends by laying two 16½-inch 1" × 8" pine boards across two of the 2" × 2" corner posts. Make sure everything is nice and square. Using a countersink bit, pre-drill for the screws, boring a ⅜-inch-deep countersink channel so that the screw's head will sink deep into the hole. Build the other end in the same manner.

Balancing the short ends using idle body parts, predrill and countersink the long facing boards, attaching them to the corner posts at both ends. Now you have the basic box. Slip the box over the three bottom boards.

Screw 'Em
Attach the bottom boards to the box using six predrilled, countersunk 1½-inch screws on each end of the trunk a half inch up from the bottom. Build the lid by laying out the two 1" × 10" boards and clamping them together. Lay the 1" × 2" strapping pieces across the two large boards roughly six inches in from each end, and then sink four one-inch screws in each piece of strapping. Bingo, you're lid-enabled.

Your own tickle trunk.

All Lidding Aside

Set the lid aside and drill two half-inch holes in each end of the trunk to hold the rope handles. Tie knots on the inside of the trunk to secure the handles in place, and cauterize them using a lighter so they won't fray.

Attach the thirty-inch piano hinge to the box along the back rim. Then use a jig or a pile of books to support the lid while attaching the hinge to the lid. Screw one end of the steel chain to the inside of the trunk and the other end to the lid of the trunk.

Crate Expectations

Hammer in the plugs to cover the screw heads. Sand and finish the chest's exterior surface with beeswax polish, or stain it if you prefer. Load that baby up with dainties and be on your chest behavior.

Panel Your Energies

Lattice panels for privacy and disguise

Lattice was invented for the times in life when you need privacy, like when you're barbecuing naked. When you think about it, lattice is ubiquitous. Lattice in confession booths lets you speak frankly without being intimidated by the priest's facial expression. And while we're on the subject of sin, what is a lacy bra but a delicate latticework designed to strategically obstruct the view?

Lattice has unlimited uses, especially in the backyard. For example, my neighbor has a beat-up old shed in his backyard. It sits right on the property line, giving off an Appalachian vibe. We asked him if we could upgrade our side of the building with some swanky lattice, and now the building looks like a high-end cabana.

Lattice is available in several styles: square, diagonal, or the "privacy" type that features very closely woven latticework. Lattice can be made from cedar, redwood, pressure-treated wood, or vinyl. My favorite kind is made from pure cedar, and it's thick enough to last fifty years. It is most commonly available in 4' x 8' sheets, and it's quite flexible and floppy unless you anchor it to something or build a frame for it.

Frame and Fortune

My favorite way to work with lattice is to frame it with a style of 2" × 4" lumber called "top rail." Top rail has a half-inch channel running right down the middle of each board, so the edge of the lattice slips inside the channel. Using top rail to frame sheets of lattice will give you individual panels that can be attached to each other; hinged together; incorporated into

Science-fiction writer Ursula K. Le Guin said, "The only thing that makes life possible is the permanent, intolerable uncertainty; not knowing what comes next." That attitude may be popular in science-fiction circles, but if you don't know what comes next in carpentry, it's no picnic. But my point is: Carpentry is a science, so why isn't there any carpentry fiction?

TIPS

• When you're measuring in preparation for cutting lattice sheets and top-rail boards, remember to account for the lattice sliding into the half-inch deep channels on all four sides! Those channels mean you lose a full inch vertically and another full inch horizontally in the finished dimensions of your framed panel.

• Buy exterior grade screws so the panels aren't rust-streaked after the first rainstorm.

screens, fences, railings, porch skirts, or pergola roofs; or anchored to buildings to disguise their appearance. Whatever you decide to do, you'll do it efficiently with lattice panels, unless you're building a boat.

If your project requires smaller panels, you can cut the lattice sheets to size. This is tricky no matter what kind of saw you use, because the material tends to vibrate, bind, split, or shoot little shards of wood into the air.

Lattice covers a multitude of sins.

Cut It Out

The best way I've found to cut lattice is to lay several 2" × 4" boards on your work surface, spaced about eighteen inches apart. Place the lattice sheet on top of the boards so it is evenly supported. Measure and mark where you want to cut. Now clamp a long board next to the marked line to provide a cutting guide and to help steady the lattice.

Wood Advice

Lattice varies in quality. Sturdier lattice is more expensive but it lasts a lifetime, so avoid the really flimsy stuff if your budget allows. When choosing your top rail in the lumber yard, check each board rigorously to make sure the channel is straight from end to end. Sometimes the channels veer off to one side, making it hugely frustrating to fit the corners together.

Once you've fit the top-rail frame around the sheet of lattice, you can prevent the lattice from twisting or bowing in the frame by tacking the lattice to the frame in several places with galvanized finish nails. Remember, lattice is a gift you give yourself for those times in life when you don't want to see or be seen, like when you're teeing off. That's why my next lattice project is a portable golf disgrace screen.

SAFETY ALERT!

• Wear safety glasses if you're using a power saw to cut lattice.

What's the Twig Deal?

A whimsical outdoor room starts with a rustic garden screen

When people first thought up hinges for doors, they made them out of leather. So what I don't understand is, when they locked a damsel in a castle tower as punishment for some misdeed, why couldn't she have just used her pocket knife to cut through the leather hinges and then bust the door down and make a daring escape?

I mean, what was the problem there?

The idea of creating an outdoor room to lounge in on summer evenings is not new. The trend started with the nomadic tribes who first wandered the continent, relaxing under the open skies beside massive barbecue pits. If only the subsequent waves of European settlers had realized how hip barbecuing would ultimately become in North America, they might have found a nicer way to fit in.

You can start creating your own romantic idyll with a few twigs and some 2×4s. In fact, this is a great project for those new to woodworking, because it's "rustic," meaning that even if your results fall somewhere between monstrous and butt ugly, you still rock.

If people criticize your garden screen, laugh mockingly and say, "It's rustic, man. It's a choice." Then try limping a little when you walk away, so they realize that things haven't always been this easy for you.

To build your garden screen you'll need one afternoon and the following stuff:

Tools
Pruning shears, knife, handsaw or power saw, drill and drill bits, pencil, scissors, clamps, leather punch or awl, goggles, gloves

Materials
Lots of freshly cut branches, 2" × 4" cedar or redwood, 3" exterior-grade wood screws, waterproof exterior-grade

wood glue, ⅜" or ½" cove molding, scrap of oil-tanned leather, 1" brass screws

TIPS

• If you want to drill a hole at an angle, it's hard to get the bit started unless you use this technique: Start by placing the drill bit perpendicular to the wood surface. Fire up the drill and let the bit sink into the wood about a quarter-inch. Then stop the motor, sharply angle the drill bit in the desired direction, and continue drilling.

You might want to grow a few vines on your screen before the naked sunbathing starts.

Branching Out

Gather up lots of recently pruned or wind-downed tree branches. Trim off the smaller growth to use in constructing your garden screen. Depending on the season, you may also find masses of fresh prunings wherever utility companies are trimming branches away from power lines. (Just ask before taking them. You never know if some utility employee is thinking about mass-producing garden screens.)

Trim all the leaves from each branch you've chosen, exposing the sculptural aspects of the branch. New growth tends to

SAFETY ALERT!

• When you're whittling, always ensure that the blade's direction of travel is *away* from you and your irreplaceable body parts.

be straighter and more flexible. Older growth has many bends and knuckles and it's more brittle.

Prep the ends of the branches by cutting them off cleanly with pruning shears. Using a sharp knife, remove a one-inch ring of bark from the ends of the branches. Whittle each branch-end into a circular shape since you want it to fit nicely into a drilled hole. Be careful not to taper the end. You want it to be cylindrical, not conical like a sharpened pencil.

Size of Contentment

Determine the size of the screen you want to build. Mine finished up six feet high with three separate panels (one three-foot-wide panel in the center, connected to two-foot-wide panels on either side).

Cut your 2" × 4" boards to length using a handsaw or power saw, and screw the corners together with exterior-grade three-inch wood screws. Predrill so the screws get started easily. Use two screws in each corner so the frame is sturdy and won't tend to rack and twist.

When you have completed the assembly of the rectangular panel, mark a dotted line all along the inside of the frame right in the center of the boards; this line will guide you when you're placing the branches along the inside of the frame.

Lay a few branches in position. Let them intersect the frame at an angle or arrange them so they're perpendicular to it. Mark the spots where the branches will be inserted.

Use your drill index to help determine the size of the hole to drill for each branch. Pull out a bit that appears to be the correct size and try pushing the branch into the drill index hole. Keep trying until you find a hole that fits the branch snugly. Use the bit from that hole to drill into the frame.

Fit Happens

Continue drilling holes and fitting branches. After dry-fitting about five branches, glue them in position using outdoor carpenter's glue. Work up one side of your panel, drilling and gluing. Then flip the frame over and work down the other side in the same manner. Once all the branches are glued in place, weave together all of the twigs that stick out, coaxing them into the flatter plane of the frame. If your branches are green enough, they should bend easily around the others, making a thick, springy mat.

Apply cove molding to trim out the inside of the frame on both faces. Cut the molding to length, giving it forty-five-degree cuts on the ends so the trim fits inside the panel like a picture frame, with nicely mitered corners. Dry-fit the trim first to make sure the lengths are accurate, and then glue it in place with exterior wood glue. Clamp the trim in position for twenty minutes while the glue sets up.

Leather Report

Leather hinges are fun to make and perfect for this application because the screen is likely to be placed on uneven ground, so the flexibility of the hinges actually stabilizes the screen. To make the hinges, cut three-inch squares of heavy leather. Then punch holes with a leather punch where the screws go. (If you don't have a leather punch, an awl or ice pick will do the job.) Predrill and screw the hinges in place using brass or other exterior-grade "pan-head" wood screws.

Now set up your garden screen. Arrange a few lawn chairs in its cozy embrace and throw a side of buffalo on the barbie. Life hasn't been this good since the 1400s.

Pot and Bothered

Making lightweight concrete pots

Kneeling in the rose bed, she reached up with graceful fingers and restrained a stray wisp of hair dancing across her silky cheek. With a soft intake of breath she thought of Edgar, the man she ached for. Then her reverie shattered as Bob the neighbor, shirtless and corpulent, fired up his riding mower.

Near the end of winter, many people become cranky. During the Renaissance, cranky people were diagnosed with "melancholia." Physicians thought melancholia was caused by too much "black bile," which sounds bad and probably didn't smell great either. I've never actually seen my own bile, but if it showed up black, that could make me pretty crabby. I'd be inclined to slap on a leech and hope I perked up a bit.

But nowadays it's hard to find a good leech in early spring. That's how I came up with my own solution for end-of-winter doldrums. This time it's not getting drunk and lying on an ice floe, although that's always a real problem-solver.

To uplift your mood, you first have to go to the bottom of your emotional pit, because the energy you're expending to avoid that pit is probably what's making you feel so rotten in the first place. I say let's just get it over with. When you want to get in touch with your inner pit, try building something complicated. This will make you confront your limitations and plunge you to the bottom of your worst mood. Once you're there, you're free. Nothing can possibly make you feel worse, so any change in your mood is going to be for the better.

If you need an idea for what to build, I suggest working with some form of concrete. Concrete is by far the most exasperating of materials, and remember, we're going for a total emotional purge here. How about building some concrete garden pots? I found recipes for a cement-based batter called hypertufa that cures to look like stone but is also lightweight enough to be moved around the patio. Once cured, it's freeze-

and thaw-proof so it can be left outside year-round. With hypertufa, you can build pots, benches, birdbaths, stepping stones, troughs, planters, fountains, faux rocks, garden sculptures, and even (if you don't trust the tastes of your loved ones) your own tombstone monument.

Basic Mixtures

The Classic: 1 part Portland cement, 1 part sand, 2 parts peat moss — gives a grey, matte finish with a rough, rustic texture.
The Smoothie: 1 part Portland cement, 1½ parts sand, 1½ parts peat moss — results in a pearly grey, smooth finish.
The Lightweight: 1 part Portland cement, 1 part peat moss, 1 part perlite, 1 part fibermesh (little pieces of fiberglass to add strength) — the lightest of the mixtures since it contains no sand; has a bumpy, lumpy texture.
The Sparkly: 1 part Portland cement, 1 part peat moss, 1 part vermiculite — quite lightweight and has a sparkly finish owing to the vermiculite.

Optional Additives

- Acrylic fortifying admixture (helps to strengthen and add flexibility to concrete products)
- Concrete dyes, pigments, and stains, available at home improvement centers and hardware stores
- Earth pigments and artists' pigments, available in art supply shops
- Iron fertilizer (makes the hypertufa go a gorgeous rusty color)

Mudder of Invention

Using a hoe, mix the dry ingredients in a wheelbarrow, adding enough water (or concrete admixture) to form a satisfying mud-pie consistency. If you're using a recipe with a high peat content, like The Classic or The Smoothie, add more moisture

TIPS

- Paint the finished pot with beer to encourage lichen and mold to grow, adding surface texture and apparent age.
- Plant moss in any cracks and crevices on the outside of the pot. Its roots will take hold in the peat.
- Put moss together with yogurt (or buttermilk) in a blender and whirl it around. Paint the resulting mixture on the outside of the pot to start moss growing all over it.

because peat is very absorbent. It leaches water from the mixture, drying it out like an overcooked meatloaf. Then your pot falls apart and so does your optimism.

Cover a mold (an existing pot, basket, tub, etc.) with a plastic garbage bag. Pat the mud batter 1½ to 2 inches thick all over the outside of the mold (for an organic, rustic-looking surface) or all over the inside walls of the mold (for a very smooth outer surface). Make the bottom as flat as possible and put a drainage hole in it.

The amazing range of hypertufa possibilities.

Sculpt decorative patterns on the outside of the pot if you like. Some people like to press the back sides of rhubarb leaves into the wet hypertufa to give the pot some decoration. When you're done, allow the pot to cure for twenty-four hours, then slip it off the mold — carefully! I've busted a few. If you wish, you can use a wire brush to give the semihardened pot a rough, pitted, stonelike finish. Let the pot cure for an additional four to six weeks, then rinse it with lots of white vinegar to remove the alkalinity and prevent lime from damaging tender plant roots.

Hang It All!

Mounting know-how

R emember in the cartoons when someone would crash into a wall and a big chunk of plaster would fall out, revealing horizontal stripes of wood? (*Trivia:* Those horizontal boards under the plaster are called lath.) Then later in the same cartoon, a character would be so scared that he'd smash right through the wall, leaving the exact outline of his silhouette behind, but they never showed the lath around the *edges* of the silhouette hole where it should have been. This drove me crazy, and I'm still not over it.

Now, let's say you need to hang a picture or mount a cabinet. Your hanging options will be determined by the

A fter you hang a lot of stuff, you feel pretty pumped and rowdy. That's when I like to imagine life on the pro wrestling circuit. One day, I'll be ready.

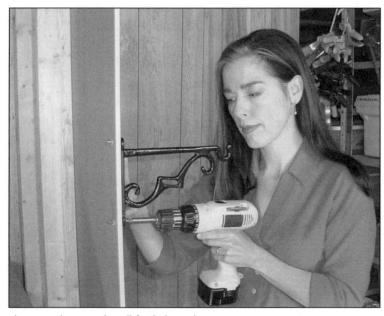

Plastic anchors work well for lighter objects.

TIPS

• In case you're wondering, this is what happens behind your wall when you install an anchor: As soon as the screw enters the inner shaft of the anchor, the anchor's nose cone blossoms into an array of plastic prongs. These prongs prevent the anchor from getting ripped out of the wall by the weight of the object, or even the weight of a small child who decides to swing on the object. (Whereas if you had screwed only into drywall, both object and child would now be lying on the floor and one of them would be upset.)

composition of your walls. Your house may have sheetrock (drywall) or lath and plaster walls, depending on its age. A house that's under forty usually has sheetrock walls, but how do you know for sure? Try inserting a thumbtack into the wall. If it sinks in easily, you've got drywall. If the thumbtack absolutely won't puncture the surface, your walls are plaster.

Mounting Enthusiasm

Hanging lightweight items on drywall is dead easy. Use a picture hook and hammer the nail through the angled channel so the density of the drywall supports it.

To hang something that's a bit heavier (up to ten pounds), install anchors. Most anchors are plastic and shaped like little projectiles with segmented nose cones that spring apart behind the wall once you drive a screw into them. Here's how to install one:

1. Drill a pilot hole to match the diameter of the anchor. To get a perfect-sized pilot hole, remove a drill bit from your drill index and drop the anchor into the index hole. If the hole doesn't fit, take out a different drill bit and test the anchor again until you find a hole that takes three-quarters of the length of the anchor, leaving the remaining quarter sticking up. Use the winning drill bit to bore your pilot hole.
2. Tap the anchor into place with a hammer.
3. Predrill a hole through the object you're hanging, then drive a screw through the object and directly into the wall anchor.

These plastic anchors work OK, and you'll find them packaged with most brackets or shelf units you buy. Technically, they're meant for masonry and concrete, not drywall, but they work. If you want the very best, throw out the tubular plastic anchors and buy the Buildex E-Z Ancor brand; they look like big plastic screws. They grip a lot better than the little tube-shaped anchors and will never pull out of the wall; plus they hold up to seventy pounds per anchor.

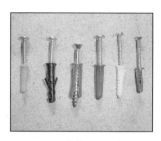

A variety of cheapy plastic anchors.

Hanging a really hefty item like a cabinet, shelf unit, or coat rack takes more diligence. You have to find at least one stud to screw into. (They never showed the studs in the cartoons either. Talk about exasperating.)

Stud Study

Studs are generally 2" × 4" boards spaced sixteen inches apart. Theoretically, if you can find one stud, you can find another every sixteen inches along the wall; realistically, this is not the case. In days of yore not all builders were fans of sixteen-inch spacing. Maybe they were stingy or lazy or both. Maybe they were drunk or measuring the intervals using body parts, but for some reason they sometimes put studs up to twenty-four inches apart. So if you find old studs in odd positions just shrug and mutter, "Those crazy drunk stud cowboys."

A sample of some Buildex E-Z Ancors.

To locate a stud you can use one of the following methods, all of which have failed at one time or another:

1. Drill a small hole, poke a wire through it, and fish around to the right and left, hoping to hit a stud. When you do hit one, attempt to place your drill bit over the correct area and drill into the stud. This takes an average of six holes.
2. Draw a horizontal line at the height you want to hang your object. Then drill a series of little holes along the line, about an inch apart, until you hit wood.
3. Walk along the wall, knocking and listening attentively for changes in pitch. Even the pros can screw this up.
4. Find an electric receptacle or switch, which is almost always attached to a stud on one side or the other. Measure from there to your hanging location using

SAFETY ALERT!

• Wear safety glasses when working with drills, hammers, screws, and nails. The tiny devils have a way of launching themselves at irreplaceable body parts.

sixteen-inch increments, from the center of the first board to the center of the next. (Try taking the receptacle cover or switchplate off and looking inside the box to see which side is attached to a stud.)

5. Use a $2 magnetic stud finder, which becomes magnetically aroused when it passes over the heads of metal nails or screws. Troll back and forth across the wall until you identify a vertical path of nails where drywall is secured to a stud.

6. Use an electronic stud finder that measures wall density and beeps enthusiastically when it passes over studs (or water pipes, which are always surprising to drill into).

Once you've located a stud, mark an X in pencil over the location. Drill a subtle test hole using a ¹⁄₁₆-inch drill bit to make sure you hit wood. (There will be telltale sawdust in the helical flutes of the drill bit.) Then predrill for your screw (optional), position your object, and drive the screw through the object right into the stud.

You must hit a minimum of one stud to take the main burden of weight. If your object is small and won't reach a second stud, use two screws stacked vertically several inches apart on the same stud, or use a wall anchor for the second screw.

Screwy Trivia

Guess how much weight it would take to snap a #8 wood screw.

   a. 150 pounds
   b. 500 pounds
   c. more than 1,000 pounds

The correct answer is c. This is called "shear strength"; screws won't shear off until there's a huge amount of weight on them. It helps to have conversation starters like this if you're ever stuck in an elevator with an attractive colleague.

Who's Got the Last Lath Now?

Hanging stuff on plaster walls

In older houses, walls are formed from lath and plaster, which is a modern version of wattle and daub, the ancient art of slapping muck (daub) on a framework of sticks (wattle), still practiced in many developing countries. The actual lath used in old buildings is narrow, splintery, rough-sawn lumber, much like the stuff they use nowadays to make snow fencing and cheap toilet paper. Lath's coarse surface was perfect for holding a drippy coat of plaster without sloughing it off. It was positioned horizontally, with narrow spaces between boards to allow the plaster to ooze through and hook behind the lath, increasing the chances of the plaster staying in place as it was applied. The plaster used in making these walls was a cement-based mixture that dried as hard as rock.

So if you decide to hang a picture and you just try to bash a nail into your plaster, two things can happen. Either chunks of wall crash to the floor or the nail ricochets off the wall and embeds itself somewhere sensitive. The trick to getting a nail into plaster without injury to your home or person is to pre-drill with a special bit called a masonry bit. This carbide tip grinds through concrete, brick, cinder block, or plaster with relative ease. You can also make do with a regular bit, but you'll just wreck it by dulling its cutting edge.

Once you've drilled through the plaster and hit wood, stop. The masonry bit is not sharp enough to drill through the wooden lath and will just grind against the wood in a futile waste of torque. Be glad you've hit wood and proceed with simply nailing your picture hook in place.

Learning to do carpentry work can be challenging. This is why it's good to work alone, especially if you talk out loud, or sometimes out very loud, using expressive language. Keep that kind of talk between you and your carpentry. This is the origin of the word "carping."

TIPS

• Drill at a forty-five-degree angle to get maximum hold.

The downside of trying to hang a picture.

You'll know when you blast through the plaster and hit air instead of wood that you've drilled into the horizontal space between two pieces of lath. Instead of using a nail, you will have to use a plastic or metal anchor. If you're hanging something heavy, drill an even bigger hole and insert a toggle bolt, a very effective kind of anchor that will hold huge amounts of weight.

If you've got something quite large, like a cabinet or shelf unit, then it pays to find the vertical studs behind the lath and screw the unit to that. Finding studs beneath lath can be a stiffer challenge than finding a flattering bathing suit. Your best bet is to use an electronic stud finder to locate the studs buried beneath the lath and plaster. However, they can be finicky and tend to confuse studs with lath, so they beep constantly and give inaccurate readings. This can be corrected by buying one of the higher-end stud finders with a Deep Scan function. The least expensive stud finder is the $2 magnetic model, which can detect vertical rows of nails where the lath is attached to the studs. Good luck drilling through that without hitting a lath nail, that's all I'll say.

Glass Backwards

Revive a busted window or convert it to a mirror

Everyone should know how to fix a broken window because projectiles happen, and behind every projectile is a surprised child, so you might as well teach your kids how to fix broken windows too. It'll save them years of allowance. If you

Two thousand years ago it was just as hard to look good as it is today, and they didn't even have mirrors. Their answer was to give mental excellence a higher value than beauty, which is probably why early multinational cosmetic conglomerates got such a slow start.

live in an apartment or condo and you never get pelted with baseballs or rocks, I know how disappointing that can be. But take heart, because you can use these glazing techniques to create a cool mirror from an old window.

Old and Bold

There's nothing quite so noble as an old window. It has a special look that says, "I've been through some stuff." Like the look of a married guy who's nearing the end of his midlife crisis and still hasn't bought a sports car or shaved his head or daydreamed about the cashier in the Dairy Queen drive-through. It's a look that says, "I can hang on a little longer, but it'd better be worth it." And that's darn attractive in a man. Or a window.

Tools

Safety glasses, gloves, putty knife, wire brush, measuring tape, glass cutter, fine-tip marker, ruler, grozing pliers (optional), glazing points

Materials

Glass or mirror, glazing compound (for window option), glass cleaner

Pane in the Glass

Whether you're fixing a single broken pane or replacing them all to make a mirror, wear safety glasses and gloves, and start removing the old putty. Depending on the acumen of the last person who fixed the window, you will probably become acutely irritated. This is because the previous fix-it enthusiast was probably winging it, so you might be chipping out rock-hard epoxy or even fossilized Play-Doh. Human ingenuity has no limits. Well, it does, but that's never stopped a handyperson.

Once you've scraped away all the putty (or unidentifiable putty alternative), carefully remove the glass from the frame.

Cut Instincts

Use a wire brush to clean up any remaining debris clinging to the frame. Next, measure the dimensions of the grooved edges that formerly held the windowpane. Subtract about ⅛-inch on both length and width so that the new glass fits loosely in the enclosure.

Cut glass to match the dimensions you need. This is fantastically easy. All you need is a $5 glass-cutting tool, which is nothing more than a handle with a tiny cutting wheel at one end. Wearing gloves, measure and mark a line on the surface of the glass (or mirror, glass side up) with a fine-tip marker, and then place a ruler alongside the line. Position the glass cutter against the edge of the ruler to ensure a straight cut. Then, putting pressure on the wheel, score a line alongside the ruler. You should hear a searing sound as the glass crystals part under the force of the wheel.

Once you've scored the line, bring the glass to the edge of the table. Place the marked line directly over the edge of the table, and then bring the overhanging glass down firmly over the edge, causing it to snap along the scored line. You might feel timid the first few times you try this, but you'll soon find it's a lark compared to trudging all the way to the hardware store to get somebody else to cut it for you.

Fits and Pieces

Drop the glass into position to check the fit. If it binds, try reducing it by gnawing on the tight edge with a pair of grozing pliers, available at stained-glass stores. Or just save that piece of glass for another section, and cut a fresh piece a tad smaller.

Lock the glass in position with glazing points (little metal wedges that are easily driven into the wood frame with a putty knife). Insert one point every four inches or so.

TIPS

• When you're getting ready to cut, run the wheel of your glass cutter through a drop of vegetable oil to lubricate it; this will make the scoring go more smoothly and minimize skipping.

• Don't run your glass cutter over the same cut twice.

• You can find old windows at building salvage supply outlets, which are all the rage in Europe and just beginning to catch on here. Great local salvage is available at Habitat for Humanity ReStores, which offer both new and used building supplies at reduced prices. Visit www.habitat.org to find one in your area.

SAFETY ALERT!

• Dispose of broken glass shards by placing them in a cardboard box or a heavy paper bag prior to depositing them in a garbage bag. This will prevent dire "poke-through" injuries for whoever takes out and picks up the garbage. Some communities may have a recycling center that takes broken glass, so make sure you check the local regulations for proper disposal methods.

OK, if you're making a mirror, you're done! Hang that baby. Strut a little. You've just acquired your own antique wood-frame mirror and saved yourself about a hundred bucks.

The Putty Professor

If you're fixing a window rather than making a mirror, this is your big chance to be a hero to the next hapless soul who busts a pane. Use real glazing compound, also known as window putty, and not some goofy alternative, like fifty-year exterior caulk or marine epoxy or Bondo.

Splendor in the glass.

Knead a ball of glazing compound in your hands until it's pliable. Roll it into a long, half-inch-thick worm, and then press the worm into the joint so it makes good contact with both the glass and the wood frame. Finally, smooth the surface of the compound with a putty knife, giving it a nice, tidy forty-five-degree angle. Remove the excess with a corner of the putty knife and clean up the window surface with glass cleaner. Glazing compound takes about a week to cure. At that point you should touch up the paint where necessary so there's no bare wood showing.

Was that fun or what? There's nothing like blasting through a project like this and then relaxing with your favorite beverage. Which reminds me, it's beer-thirty.

Fire and Ice

Make a mini-fireplace for winter

If you're like most of us, you probably get a fat bottom during the winter. It spills over the edges of your chair, more dimpled by the day. Experts say this is caused by lack of exercise, but they're wrong. Fat bottoms are caused by pride. You have the ski equipment. You have the skates. But you haven't used any of your gear in years, because you're worried you'd wipe out. But in actual fact, you would. Just know that being humiliated on the slopes and rinks is a winter tradition. It's character-building. It gives us the ability to look one another in the eye and say, "I'm not even wearing long johns." That's because you had to take them off after you got so hot from wiping out and getting back up again.

It's hard not to take things personally when you're working alone, because if there's a problem, there's a good chance that you had something to do with it. That's why it's good to work with substandard lumber. Then there's always something to blame.

I once crashed so many times on an intermediate ski run that the ski patrol guys wound up following me down the hill with a stretcher. The friends I was skiing with pretended they didn't know me after my sixth face-plant. Then I fell off the T-bar into a stream and was stuck there for an hour. Strangers called out helpful instructions from the lift as they went by, again and again. After it was over, we relaxed in the chalet by the fire. Our cheeks were berry-red, and so were our faces.

Sitting around the fire is what makes winter worthwhile. In the dim, flickering firelight, you know you look good. Even as your extremities tingle from frostbite and your muscles occasionally jerk uncontrollably, you feel sexy. This is completely in your own mind, but it has to start somewhere. More crazy spontaneous couplings occur in ski lodges than you should probably contemplate right now. Think about it later when you've got free time.

Firelight is the reward that everyone deserves for going outside in winter. If you don't have a fireplace, you can still have your own cozy interlude in the glow of a romantic wood and copper wall sconce.

A glimmer of firelight to warm the cockles.

Tools

Speed square, saw, clamps, hammer, tin snips, drill

Materials

1" × 6" pine, stained or unstained (or any beat-up old board if you want a rustic look), carpenter's glue, copper sheeting, sheet metal screws, plumber's tape

Steps

1. Make a frame with forty-five-degree miter joints. Mark the forty-five-degree angles using a speed square, and then saw on the line. If your joints don't come out perfectly, thicken the glue with sawdust to fill the gaps. Then clamp the glued edges together while the adhesive cures. If you want, you can paint the frame to look like a brick fireplace with a tiny mantle across the top, but that would probably look really bad. I have these wacky ideas and I should know by now not to mention them. But wait, you could crochet tiny stockings to hang on the tiny mantle at Christmas. OK, I'm stopping.

2. Once the frame is done, make a gently rounded reflector using copper sheeting, which is soft and easy to work with. Roll the copper over a log to give it texture, or hammer it on an uneven surface. The more bumps and divots you make in the copper, the more the candlelight will dance and sparkle as you wrangle friskily on the bearskin rug.

3. Using a scrap of copper, cut a little shelf with a ¾-inch tab. This will hold a couple of tea-light candles. Attach the shelf, feeding the tab through two parallel horizontal slits made in the reflector. Attach the completed reflector to the rear of the frame using sharp sheet-metal screws that will easily sink into the soft copper sheeting.

4. Add support pieces so you can hang the sconce without crushing the reflector. Cut two boards from the same material

A close-up of the horizontal slits and tab as seen from the back of the reflector.

you used for the frame. Make them a bit shorter than the height of your frame; the proportions will look more artistic.

5. Predrill and then nail through the front of the frame to secure the two vertical pieces to the frame at the top and bottom.

6. To hang your sconce, cut two 1½-inch pieces of plumber's tape (metal strapping with little holes in it) and screw them to the back of the vertical supports near the top. Hang the mini-fireplace on two well-anchored nails or screws. Light your tea-lights. Don't forget marshmallows.

Sincere, but Forgot to Shop?

A last-minute handmade gift

When you make something with your hands, it doesn't matter how it turns out; you still get to brag. Stand around pointing at your project and say stuff like, "Yep, made it from scratch. Thought that one up myself, no help at all." And when onlookers are speechless, it's fair to assume they're totally impressed.

As Christmas closes in and you still haven't done any shopping, a weird thing happens. You lose your judgment. For instance, you want to give something to your buddies at work. A box of deep-fried macaroons would be a perfect reminder of all those cholesterol-soaked lunches you've shared in the past year. Too bad you forgot to pick them up at the macaroon specialty shop in early December, and now all they have left are green ones. If you'd bought the green macaroons three weeks ago, they would seem OK as a gift, because technically, you had thought ahead. But now it's late in the season, and the fact that you don't have anything for your co-workers means you have to get something really nice to make up for the fact that you don't have anything yet.

That's what I mean by "losing your judgment." These are the same co-workers who, three weeks ago, deserved green macaroons. Now you're considering leather desk accessories and cashmere PalmPilot protectors, because you don't want anyone to know how late you left it.

Don't kid yourself. They *will* know, because everyone knows the truth about Christmas shopping: the later you leave it, the more you spend. You didn't care enough to shop early, but you don't want anyone to guess you didn't care, so you spend way more than necessary.

Your options are to go elbow-to-elbow with the other lowlifes who didn't shop early, or stay at home and go with a saner option. My favorite last-minute gift is candles appliquéd with flowers pressed instantly using a microwave flower press. You may need to pick up a couple of supplies, but it's way better than joining the wriggling throngs of panicky consumers at the mall.

Flower-Encrusted Candles

Tools
Microwave flower press ($29.95, Lee Valley Tools, www.leevalley.com), ½" paintbrush

Materials
Newspapers and paper towels, natural-colored beeswax in either sheets or chunks (available at craft stores), tin pie plate for melting beeswax, fresh flowers, pine needles, cedar, rosehips or leaves, big candles (at least 4" in diameter)

The key item you need for this project is the microwave flower press, a kiln-fired pair of terra-cotta slabs measuring 6" × 6". This smart little unit presses flowers in less than two minutes (instead of the three weeks it takes in a traditional press) and preserves the colors brilliantly.

TIPS

• If you're making the candle for a guy, use screws, nuts, and bolts instead of flowers, and he'll have his own workshop candle for screwing emergencies.

• Try carving designs on the surface of candles using a chip-carving knife or a traditional V-tool, available at craft stores and woodworking suppliers. Carving wax is way easier than carving wood, so it's a great project for beginner carvers. You can carve geometric patterns, or your company logo (ick), or curly ivy vines. Then if you're really hotdogging, use a contrasting color of beeswax to paint in the lines you've carved.

A microwave press dries flowers in less than two minutes.

Steps

1. Put on some Christmas music and pour yourself a libation.

2. Count on making a mess. Arrange newspapers and paper towels on the kitchen counter to catch waxy drips.

3. Melt beeswax in a tin pie plate. The reason I use beeswax and not paraffin is that it's more stretchy and gooey, so it makes a nice flexible seal for the flowers. Paraffin tends to chip, crack, and crumble when used as an appliqué medium.

4. Start pressing flowers. Roses take about two minutes. More delicate flowers or leaves may take only one minute.

5. Dip your paintbrush into the hot, melted beeswax and dab it over the back of a pressed flower. While the wax is still warm and sticky, press the flower onto the surface of the candle. Then paint lots more hot wax over the surface of the flower so it's preserved under a layer of wax.

6. When you've finished covering the candle with flowers, paint over any blank spots with more beeswax so the whole candle is the same texture and color.

The world's greatest literature was written by candlelight.

When it comes down to it, a really homely candle is a lot nicer to receive than green macaroons or even a monogrammed aromatherapy mouse pad.

The Taming of the Shoe

A well-heeled rack for under twenty dollars

Some people think stuff only looks good if it's slick and symmetrical. But I think something a bit odd-looking can be good too. For one thing, you never get tired of it because no matter how long you have it, you still can't get used to it.

Did you know that in fifteenth-century Spain some bone-head fashionista came up with three-foot-high platform shoes? Women went mad for these shoes, even though they required two helpers just to walk. Now, as a practical woman, you're probably thinking, Why would anyone want to be hobbled by three-foot platforms?

The answer to that question reveals the true weirdness of human nature. Fifteenth-century women wanted to be incapacitated by fashion because being rendered helpless by expensive clothing sent a strong message to observers that the wearer could not possibly manage a physically demanding task. And why was that relevant? Because rich people didn't need to work. Ever. So restrictive clothing doubled as a signal of wealth and status.

This irony is present in today's fashion trends as well. The other day I watched a willowy, platform-wearing teenager trying to run for a bus. She was moving as fast as she could. I clocked her at five yards in two minutes. Her high-status platforms made her miss the bus. Technically, she was duped by fashion, because if the whole point of wearing trendy footwear is to look aristocratic, she shouldn't really be riding the bus; she should have a chauffeur.

So I think the answer to fashion, which can encourage us to appear helpless, is to treat it with bemused indulgence while simultaneously amassing a vast arsenal of tools, and then using those tools to be anything but helpless. Here's a great weekend project to practice your new skills: a shoe rack to handle footwear buildup in closets. Made from inexpensive "gingerbread" trim, the rack gives you two layers of shoes, effectively doubling closet floor space (and self-sufficiency).

Kabuki gingerbread.

Tools
Measuring tape, pencil, saw, square, clamp, drill, ½" drill bit or ½" Forstner bit, tube cutter

Materials
One piece of "gingerbread" trim (available at home improvement centers), 8' of ½" copper pipe

Cut Your Stuff
First, measure and make a mark at the center of your piece of gingerbread trim. Saw through the mark with a jigsaw, chop saw, circular saw, or handsaw. Once you've cut your gingerbread in half, figure out the best angle of tilt and the ideal spacing between the two pipes that will carry the upper

TIPS

• When you're deciding on the spacing for the copper pipe, make sure the pipes will be close enough together to catch the toes of high-heeled shoes! It's off-putting when the shoe tips fall through the rack because the pipes are a bit too far apart.

row of shoes. Lay different shoes sideways against the gingerbread, tilting them until you locate the best insertion points for the pipes that will support heels and toes. Mark those points on the wood surface.

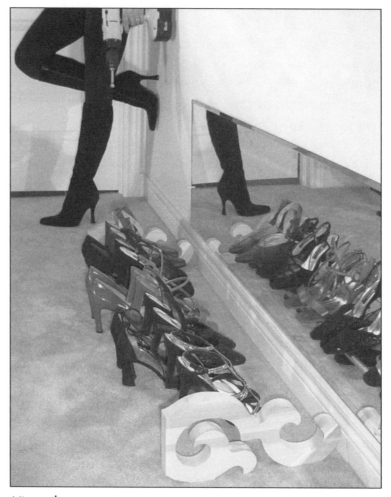

Nice rack.

Clamping Out

Next, lay the two pieces of gingerbread side by side, as though you were putting the original piece back together again.

Transfer the pipe-insertion marks that you made on the first piece to the matching half. (Use a square to measure, making sure the pairs of holes will line up accurately.) Clamp the wood pieces to your work surface. Drill ¾-inch deep holes using a ½-inch-diameter Forstner bit, which is a very clean-cutting, high-status bit; you'll be swollen with pride to own one. Of course, if you're not a flaming tool geek, a regular ½-inch drill bit works fine.

Pipe Dreams

Cut your copper pipe to length using a tube cutter, an effective little gadget found in the plumbing aisle. Copper pipe is a bit flexible across a wide span, so you'll find that you can't have an endlessly long shoe rack. You're pretty much limited to about four feet in width, depending on the weight of your shoes, unless you add a center support (an additional piece of drilled gingerbread threaded onto the pipes and positioned in the middle of the span).

Finally, insert the two copper pipes into the holes and load your rack with shoes. Then, just for contrast, strut around your new shoe rack wearing restrictive clothing *and* twirling your drill. Talk about having the best of both worlds.

Clock It to Me

Making unforgettable timepieces

In the old days, there was a saying: "Into many a homemade gift are woven loving thoughts that make the gift priceless." But nowadays if someone looks at something you've made and says, "That's priceless!" you know never to give them a homemade gift again.

They say time waits for no man, which isn't fair considering men wait for women quite a bit. This happens because men measure time in units of actual time, whereas women measure time in units of potential. For example, a man with a list of five tasks can determine that his itinerary will take him three hours to complete. Whereas a woman with twenty-five items on her list concludes that she has time to get them all done in half an hour. If a man and woman attempt to do their errands together, time becomes elastic. This is because two temporal realities move away from each other at the speed of spite. For instance, men are often ready to go out the door while women are still on the phone with their mother.

Because women deal in potentialities rather than actualities, men become impatient with women. But men should be grateful, because women's ability to see potential leads to marriage. Women believe that the men they marry will change, just as men believe that their wives will stay the same. Change is easy for women. For example, without even trying I am larger and more opinionated than I was on my wedding day. Who knew?

This temporal dysfunction exists between men and women because in general things are harder for men, so they've learned to allow extra time. For example, men's bikes have that extra bar that goes between the seat and the handlebars. This means they can't just slide on. They have to get the bike moving, balance on one pedal, and then throw the opposite leg dramatically in the air. Badly executed, this can mean a five- or six-second delay in the schedule. Men account for that. On the other hand, a woman gets easily on her bike and just rides off. You'd think she'd beat the man to the destination with this head start, but the woman has probably assumed the chain guard will work. So when her pant leg gets caught in the front sprocket and she attempts to free her leg but instead gets the tire caught in a streetcar track and arrives at her destination carrying the bike with only half her pants left, she is usually late.

If you can make a hole in it, you can make a clock out of it.

TIPS

• Use a protractor to mark each hour thirty degrees apart, or you can use your geometry know-how to divide the circle into twelve equal parts.

• Cut out a disk of sheet metal and grind the surface with a stone-grinding bit to get a slick, modern, brushed-metal effect.

• If you're making a clock out of lumber, clamp the wood down and use a hole-saw bit to cut the edges of the crater you need to hold the clockwork. Then hollow out the inside of the circle using a sharp chisel.

Physicists have discovered that if you exist in a reality in which time is measurable, then you must also contend with space. This was the origin of the expression, "If you've got the time, I've got the place." This usually turns out to be true, as I learned in university when I was assigned a single room in the dorm.

What I'm trying to say is, why not give people clocks this Christmas to remind them that time is extremely subjective? To prove this, here are some meaningful treasures I've seen made into clocks: a souvenir goose lawn ornament; a ukulele; plastic novelty vomit; a bust of Elvis; and a bedpan. The mind reels, doesn't it? Yet, all you really need to know is where to get clock kits (woodworking suppliers, some craft shops) and how to drill a hole for the clock stem, and the world is your perpetual oyster.

Make sure you measure the thickness of the material you're using for a clock face so you'll know precisely how long the clock stem needs to be. The clock stem connects the mechanism at the back to the hands at the front. The hands, available in many styles, will easily pop onto the stem. You can even buy pendulums if you want a more traditional look for your clock.

Here's a quick primer for drilling holes in various mediums:

Acrylic or polycarbonate: Use a plastic tapping bit, available from industrial plastic suppliers.
Ceramic: Use a glass/tile drill bit, available in all hardware stores.
Concrete: Use a masonry bit with a hammer drill, a heavy-duty power tool that pounds as well as grinds.
Metal: Use carbide-tipped drill bits for sheet metal, or a cobalt drill bit for thicker plate metal. You may want to lubricate with a little cutting oil, since the bit gets quite

warm. Also, make a dimple in the metal first using a hammer and nail or a compression punch, so you can start drilling without the bit skating around.

Wood: Use a normal carbon steel drill bit. You'll also need sharp chisels to mortise a hole the clock motor will sit in.

You don't really need to mark the hours on your clock face if you like to live on the edge. But if you prefer not to be guessing, you can mark them with nails, stick-on numbers, paint, or nail polish (or invisible ink if you're wryly philosophical). Don't forget the battery.

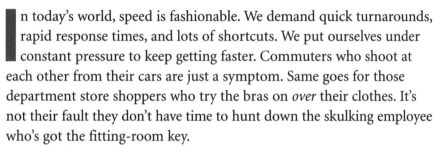

5 TOOLS AND EQUIPMENT

I n today's world, speed is fashionable. We demand quick turnarounds, rapid response times, and lots of shortcuts. We put ourselves under constant pressure to keep getting faster. Commuters who shoot at each other from their cars are just a symptom. Same goes for those department store shoppers who try the bras on *over* their clothes. It's not their fault they don't have time to hunt down the skulking employee who's got the fitting-room key.

Our culture is a training camp for impatience. When we're confronted with something that is happening slowly, we become unstable. We're unable to cope with the ancient rhythms of driving a 1989 Plymouth, or lining up at the passport office, or having a tattoo removed. We should take a lesson from the trees, who are happy to stand patiently in one place for years. Mind you, this is the reason lumber is so expensive; trees are paid by the hour.

It's important to question the need for speed and to find a few activities we can practice doing slowly and thoughtfully. The key is finding the right activity. You wouldn't want to practice slow sex. You might lose interest and fall asleep. Drinking slowly just means being not quite drunk enough for way too long. In my crowd, you earn more respect for chugging a beer and passing out.

We need to practice slowing down, and one of the best ways is working with hand tools. But if you need a quick fix for your speed addiction, you have the option of power tools. With power tools you can make more projects, more often, at ten times the speed. The only problem is, it's easier to engage the motor of a power tool than it is to engage, say, your brain. Therefore, you can make more mistakes, more often, at ten times the speed.

If we can't defeat our addiction to speed, maybe what we all need is a seminar called "Serenity through Power Tools." Because after using a hammer drill for a few minutes, your hands are totally numb. And that's as close to serenity as some of us will ever get.

Living Toolishly

Building your first and forever tool kit

My advice to new homeowners is this: Never hold back on tools. Set aside your allowance to invest in great tools. Tools will enhance your homeowning experience and protect you from Home-Moaner syndrome, wherein tool deprivation causes helplessness, remorse, and large repair bills.

You can't change a man, but you can always freshen up a furnace filter.

A real fixer-upper, and it's all mine.

Tools take us back to our hominid origins, when we roamed the plains looking for grubs and a good pounding rock. When men were hairy and women liked it. When we chose our dates by grabbing them around the neck and mounting them. This cut down on decision making, which was good because life was short.

TIPS

• If you're left-handed, try a Lee Valley (www.leevalley.com) right-to-left tape measure. It'll save you lots of exasperation.

Life is still short today, but we have the illusion of life stretching on forever, because we spend so much time convincing ourselves that we're getting the best deal, best options, best price, and best gene pool. All this calculating cuts into the time we actually have to do anything. So twenty years from now a lot of us are going to be disappointed in where we are because of what we're doing right now. Don't let this happen to you. If it does, overcompensate with a huge, fully stocked workshop in which to spend your golden years avoiding regret.

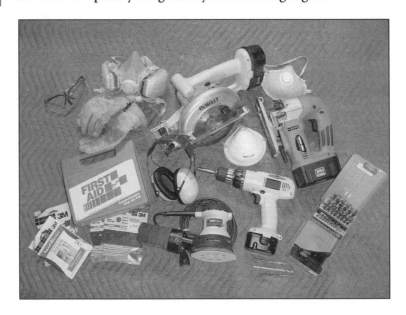

My favorite power tools and accessories.

Here is a full basic tool kit for the do-it-yourself enthusiast:

Power Tools

Circular saw: If you're into building decks or framing sheds or cutting up lots of plywood, a circular saw is best to use because it's faster than a jigsaw. I love the battery-powered models where you don't have to worry about cutting the power cord in half. You can get some nice kits that include a cordless circular saw, drill, charger, and two batteries. Oh, baby.

Cordless drill: So cool, you'll want to set an extra place at the table for it. Choose a variable speed, keyless-chuck model with the capacity to hold ⅜-inch bits (for lighter use) or ½-inch bits (for heavier use). Cordless drills are available in a wide range of battery sizes, from seven volts to thirty volts. Most people are permanently happy with a twelve-volt model.

Jigsaw: An electric jigsaw is the only power saw I recommend to beginners. Quiet and surprisingly versatile, the jigsaw makes straight or curvy cuts in wood, metal, or plastic, so your options are endless. It's easier to control and safer than any other kind of power saw. It can cut straight lines as well as a circular saw if you clamp a straightedge in place and let the jigsaw's sole plate ride along its edge, making a clean, precise cut. Jigsaws are slower than table saws, miter saws, and circular saws, but you get to keep your fingers.

Random orbit sander: More powerful and versatile than a standard electric palm sander, a random orbit sander removes material much more quickly than a palm sander because it spins as well as vibrates. It also provides vacuuming services by sucking dust up through the holes in the sanding disk and storing it in a built-in vacuum bag. Choose variable speed if you can afford it.

Safety gear: Don't even be tempted by power tools if you're not going to buy the safety gear to go with them.

- Dust masks: Get the best you can afford; the style with two elastics are better because they grip your face firmly.
- Ear protectors: A good set of ear gear will keep you calm when turning on loud, nerve-shattering equipment and will protect your hearing as well. My favorite ear protectors are made by Peltor, the brand used in many police firing ranges; they really cut the decibels. Get two pairs in case a relative is either helping you or is way past the point of listening to you bragging about your new power tools.
- Safety glasses: Buy an extra pair for a helper.

My favorite hand tools.

Hand Tools

Bastard file: This is an endlessly useful but unfortunately named metal file that's great for sharpening garden tools, de-burring metal pipe, etc.

Hacksaw: For cutting metal shelving, rigid plastic tubing, metal pipes, etc.

Hammer: For heavy-duty use, the 16-ounce (or 20-ounce, if you like more heft) antivibration hammer from Stanley has nice balance and prevents repetitive strain injuries by absorbing shock. If you just need a hammer for small household jobs like hanging pictures, Lee Valley makes a lovely eight-ounce claw hammer for the kitchen drawer.

Handsaw: Japanese handsaws are sweet to use. Cutting occurs on the pull stroke; this means the blade doesn't jam or warp (as does a Western saw blade when it is pushed through a piece of wood). Japanese saws have a very thin blade. The narrower blade with tight-set teeth cuts less wood and takes less effort too. The handle is long, allowing it to be braced along the forearm for greater control and stability. They're way easier to use than standard push saws.

Pliers: There are four styles that serve different purposes. Build your collection to include needle-nose pliers (with a wire-cutter function) for delicate work, tongue-and-groove pliers for gripping nuts and pipe fittings, lineman's pliers and wire strippers for electrical work.

Pry bars/cat's paws: These are standard tools great for demolition and quick removal of errant nails.

Putty knives: They come in a range of sizes and are versatile tools for paint scraping, caulk removal, and cocktail stirring.

Screwdrivers: Start to accumulate assorted ergonomic-grip square-head, Phillips (the one with the $\times$), and slot-head screwdrivers. Lee Valley makes a screwdriver set called Lifetime screwdrivers, which are very good and cost only about fifty bucks for the set. A word about materials: A slick plastic handle will get sweaty and slippery, and all your strength will go into squeezing rather than pushing and turning, whereas a textured or rubbery composite handle will make your job go more smoothly. If you're tight on storage space, go for an interchangeable, multibit screwdriver.

Utility knife: Get a sturdy model and avoid the lightweight versions with snap-off blades.

Wrench: If you don't already have one, get an adjustable wrench — it's a classic.

Accessories

Abrasives: Steel wool, sandpaper in incremental grits, and 3M SandBlaster abrasive pads.

Adhesives: Carpenter's glue (the yellowy stuff), Super or Krazy glue, and Loctite Power Grab, a trigger-dispensed latex-based glue that can be tinted with acrylic artist's colors to match any material.

Caulking gun: Get a professional model. It won't raise your blood pressure by jamming or dripping uncontrollably. Or skip the gun entirely and buy Loctite Press and Seal, a new style of caulk that has a built-in, automatic dispensing trigger and will add years to your life.

Clamps: Own at least one matching pair of glorious Quick-Grip clamps. It's like giving yourself a third hand, and we all know how useful that can be.

Drill index: A selection of standard carbon steel bits organized in incremental order, for drilling into wood.

Drywall mud pan and drywall knives: four-inch taping knife, plus eight-, ten-, and twelve-inch finishing knives. *Hint:* Carbon steel rusts out after the first use, so go for stainless-steel drywall accessories.

Duct tape: If you're modest about your handiwork, get 3M's new transparent duct tape and nobody will even know the repair happened.

Electronic stud sensor: Solve all your mounting emergencies with the reliable stud finder. Available in various sizes and capacities, some stud sensors even scan for pipes and electrical conduit too.

Extension cords: Heavy-duty twelve- or fourteen-gauge. Buy the shortest length you can get away with, since the longer the cord, the greater the chance of burning out the motor of your power tool.

Fasteners: Store a selection of screws, drywall anchors, finish nails, and picture hooks in lidded, transparent organizer trays.

First-aid kit: For the usual mishaps.

Level: I would suggest a torpedo level's nine inches of delight for small projects like mounting shelves. You can get a longer level (up to eight feet) for big projects like patios or retaining walls.

Lubricants: WD-40, graphite powder, petroleum jelly, and a paraffin or beeswax candle will give you lots of options when something is stuck.

Manual: A decent home-repair manual based on your level of ambition.

Masonry bits: Any time you have to drill into concrete, plaster, or masonry, you'll need a selection of carbide-tip masonry bits. If you overheat them, they turn black and then they won't work any more, so cool your bit periodically by dipping it in a bowl of polyethylene glycol (antifreeze). Masonry bits are the key to mounting shelves on basement cinder block, hanging a hose reel on brick, and drilling into ossified plaster walls.

Measuring tape: They say that if you've got big hands it means you must have a big tape, but I find thirty-foot tape awkward and bulky. If you're not building houses or large projects, a shorter tape is sufficient. I like the fit of a sixteen-footer in my hand, with a twelve-footer in my purse just for backup.

Nail sets: They come in a package of three different head sizes and allow you to sink nail heads tidily beneath the wood surface.

Respirator mask: For blocking petrochemical vapors, solvents, etc.

Speed square: A crucial triangular tool for marking and cutting lumber, squaring shelves, etc.

Stepladder: A six-foot stepladder will solve most of your height issues.

Work gloves: One pair of leather gloves for heavy, dirty work; one pair of rubber gloves for handling concrete products; and a box of latex disposable gloves for painting and other messy jobs.

For Whom the Belt Tools

The importance of owning a tool belt

Sometimes you want to do peaceful, constructive things. Other times you want to make a lot of noise and bust stuff up. That's what I like about hormones: infinite variety with no danger of boredom.

If you're looking for a hot little outfit to spice up your domestic life, don't spend money on lingerie. Invest in a tool belt. Some women avoid tool belts because they're afraid of looking bulky. This never occurs to men, who describe women in tool belts as "hot."

Why do guys think that a hulking, tool-stuffed belt makes a woman look hot? Guys don't need much help thinking that women are hot, plus they're excited by the confidence radiating from the tool-belt wearer. In surveys, most men rate confidence as the most important quality in women whom they consider attractive.

My husky belt.

My extra-husky belt.

Why does the tool-belt wearer feel confident? Because she's got important things banging against her thighs with every step she takes. In her own mind, she's striding forward in slow motion, glistening with sweat, in a panoramic tilt-shot of the heroine at the triumphant end of some postapocalyptic action flick.

Choosing a Tool Belt

Tool belts come in two styles; husky and extra-husky. If you go to the tool-belt section of your home improvement center or hardware store, you'll spot the extra-husky belts right away, because that's all they carry. These belts cost upwards of $80, and have many stout pouches that will impede your egress through most doorways. The pouches are usually leather or Cordura nylon and are built for infinity. They're heavy too, so a fully loaded belt can drag on your sacrum and give you lower-back discomfort. There are much better ways to get lower-back discomfort, so avoid this one. In fact, you may want to eschew the tool-belt section of the hardware store altogether and opt for the customized husky belt.

Customizing a Tool Belt

The husky has the slimmest profile available in a tool belt, and here's how to get yours. Go to the gardening section of your hardware store and select a nylon gardener's belt (cheap at around $20). Make sure the pockets are looped onto the belt, not riveted permanently in place, so you can move the pockets around until you're happy with the configuration. On your way to the cashier, stop by the tool-belt section and choose a hammer hook from the assortment of stand-alone pouches and add-ons. Try it on your belt to make sure it fits.

When you get home, put on tight jeans and a T-shirt. Pull some pockets off the belt and slide the hammer hook on, and

---

TIPS

• A note of caution to women: A woman wearing a tool belt for the first time may develop temporary manly behaviors, called "mannerisms." These include grunting, phantom jock itch, and hocking loogies. Hardware psychologists are not sure why this happens. But when you think about it, wearing a tool belt is the closest a woman will ever come to knowing what it's like to be a guy. All those dangly bits hanging off us are a huge distraction, just like real dangly bits are for guys. So don't be surprised if you find yourself strutting in front of a mirror and comparing your hammer size to others'.

then replace the pockets. Snap that baby on and load up. Feel the swagger come into your step. Arrange the pockets so they disguise any body parts that may not be as perky as you now feel.

Dressed to Drill

Stuff to know about your new best friend

A drill has so much personality that you might find yourself talking to yours. You might even feel maternal toward it, or coach it in a friendly way, or tell it about the time when you kissed that guy but then he never called you. When you reach that level of friendship with your drill, it's best to work alone for a while, because that's how rumors get started.

You can pay big money for a self-esteem seminar, or you can buy yourself a cordless drill. I recommend the drill. For one thing, it's cheaper. For another thing, if it doesn't work, you get your money back. Besides, you can wear your drill in a holster on your belt, and if that doesn't scream, "I know who I am, and I'm learning to deal with it," I don't know what does.

Strap on a holster and you'll be amazed at the feeling you get from a six-pounder grazing your thigh. You'll walk like someone who's looked into the jaws of eternity and seen that it's got tonsils, just like everyone else. You'll be able to face your high-school reunion, knowing you're packing the kind of action your jeans had back when you were sixteen. Or if you're around forty and you suddenly realize you've never had a baby, you can find solace in a cordless drill. There are many parallels. People will want to hold it, coo over it, and they'll like the way it smells.

Choosing a drill is much like choosing a mate: you want one that's going to last the rest of your life, no matter what you put it through. You also want one that will make it unnecessary to look at other models that enter the market. Occasionally, some girls want more than one at a time, and

The thrill of the drill.

If you would like a deeper understanding of the word "torque," here it is:

• Torque is a twisting force, the kind needed to tighten a screw. If there is no torque acting on a screw, its angular momentum is a constant. In the same way, if there is no torque acting on your body when you do yoga, you need a tighter leotard.

• If somebody applies torque to a screw with a large cordless drill, the angular momentum of the screw is still constant, relative to the force from the cordless drill. This is a roundabout way of saying that constant screwing over a long period of time really has no consequences on either body, unless one of them is overweight.

(continued on p. 184)

that's pure torment. Try to avoid it. After all, it's just screwing. Let's keep it in perspective.

The day you go to the hardware store to choose your drill is a day you'll remember forever, so dress accordingly. You may feel a prickle of anxiety, which is normal. You may feel mild arousal, which is abnormal. Know the difference.

There are three things to look for in your cordless drill: variable speed, a keyless chuck, and the proper weight for your size and strength.

TIPS

(continued from p. 183)
• Having higher torque means the screwing will go faster. Therefore, in some cases, lower torque may actually be desirable. Not so low that you're going to fall asleep, but high enough to keep you from wondering if you should be answering that phone.

Variable Speed

If you lightly depress the trigger on a drill and it jumps to blazing speed with no warning, you are not holding a variable speed drill. Variable speed means the drill operates like a sewing machine, so that light pressure on the trigger makes it run quite slowly, and more pressure speeds it up.

Using a drill that doesn't have variable speed is harder on your self-esteem than going to a bad hairdresser, and then deciding not to go to her anymore, and just when your hair is looking really dire, you run into her at the mall and she gives you that look like you're a dork. So you book another appointment with her right then and there, and then later you phone and cancel with a lame excuse like "I have shingles."

Keyless Chuck

Many drills come equipped with keyless chucks, and so should yours. With a keyless chuck you don't need a little steel key to tighten and untighten the gripping tines. A keyless chuck is usually made from high-impact plastic and has ribbing that makes it easy to grip. Holding the chuck while reversing the drill lets you loosen and remove a bit, whereas gripping the chuck and running the drill in "forward" tightens a bit in place. This is a much more efficient way to work than using a nasty key that is easily lost. A keyless chuck allows for finesse and speed that others will see as catlike sensuality.

Proper Weight

The weight of your drill depends on the size of the battery it's sporting. Batteries range in capacity from light-duty purse models (seven volts) all the way up to heavy-duty beefcakes (twenty-four volts). For most people, a twelve-volt cordless drill is a great all-around tool with plenty of torque and versatility.

You may want to sleep with your new drill under your pillow for the first couple of nights. This is normal. Just remove the battery so that if you roll over on it, there are no surprises.

It's Not How You Feel; It's How You Look

Repair apparel for the modern miss, mister, and ma'am

One birthday a bunch of my friends pitched in and bought me a $400 Donna Karan top. It was a tiny, figure-hugging piece of finery. I traded it in for a six-person tent with a rainfly and skylights. I've had way more fun in my tent than I would've had in my Donna Karan top. For one thing, I can get someone else in there with me. For another thing, the tent accommodates many geographical circumstances, whereas the Donna Karan top compressed valuable topography.

If the Donna Karan top had had half the features of my tent, I would never have traded it in. Fashion designers ignore the modern girl's desire for multipurpose clothes. Clothes that have adjustable waistlines, secret pockets, and lots of zippers for easy access to important locations. Clothes that are ladylike yet don't show the beer stains. Clothes that make us feel at home under the sink, on top of the riding mower, or in a 1970s rock band. I'm talking about a flattering set of coveralls.

You can make your own coveralls if you can sew. Home ec wasn't my strongest subject, but it wasn't Mrs. Robertson's fault that I sewed the sleeves onto my dress upside down, and then the only way to wear it was to keep both arms straight up in the air. I still have that dress for days when I want to appear enthusiastic.

TIPS

• Great coveralls and jumpsuits can be ordered through the Internet from various places, including www.dickies4less.com. Instantly, you'll feel more competent, and the bloating is gone. Live the dream.

Coveralls can be worn over anything or over nothing. They disguise or reveal, based on your ability to operate a zipper. They come off as easily as they go on. And what man doesn't dream of being ravaged in the garden shed by a coverall-doffing vixen, even if she's his wife?

Coveralls for the active miss.

Coveralls are the ultimate garment for plumbing, yoga, or swimming in leech-prone areas. If you feel like firing up the grill, coveralls are available in flame-retardant material, and if you buy them at a military surplus store, you might even get a pair with a breast-pocket nametag that says Gordo or Wilf.

Coveralls come in a wide range of attitudes, from insouciant to piquant. For example, aviator's flight-suit coveralls have saucy drawstrings at the pant cuffs, reminding us of how far we've come since the days when married girls installed privacy drawstrings in the hems of their nighties.

Once you own a pair of coveralls, you're equipped for the following situations:

- When the doorbell rings and you're in your underwear
- When chugging beer
- When visiting a car dealership (people will think you work there, so they'll leave you alone)
- When visiting a hospital (people will think you work there, so you can get free oral swabs)
- When you're self-diagnosed as "morbidly obese"

In Scandinavia, cultured university students wear coveralls to classes, to bars, to sporting events. Designer Geoffrey Beene has called them the "evening dresses of the future." People devote entire websites to coveralls and their upscale cousins, jumpsuits. Once you own a pair, you'll see why that's not weird.

Saw and Order

Choosing the best handsaw

When greeting someone socially, it's always hard to know what the other person is coming in for — a hug or a kiss or both. You have a split second to interpret which gesture is imminent before things get awkward or somebody gets hurt.

In many hardware stores, there's an impenetrable tradition of acting, thinking, and talking like it's 1910 and if you're in a hurry, that's your problem. The reason things are slowed down in hardware stores is because most of these folks have made lots more mistakes than you have, and that's why they know that taking your time is the first priority. And that's kind of a comforting attitude in our culture. Even if you want to kill them for it. And that's your problem too.

Some people clearly prefer the kissing style of greeting, and I try to cooperate. However, if one party has an overbite, tooth-to-tooth contact is likely. (This is much like head-to-faucet contact when washing your hair in the sink; your head ricochets off the porcelain a few times before you get your bearings.) Controlling your approach speed helps minimize toothy collisions.

Hugging is simpler since teeth are normally not involved. Positioning is all-important. Decide whether to use the overhand grip (arms around the person's neck) or the underhand grip (arms around their waist). The overhand grip is more intimate. The arms reach around the neck of the other person, pulling them into a full-contact embrace. The overhand grip is usually reserved for intimate friends who are unlikely to struggle. The underhand style of hug can last longer because it's comfortable indefinitely, as was proven in the encounter groups of the 1980s. But length can be wrong in a social greeting, unless you're planning to get a room.

This brings us to choosing a saw. In striking parallel with social greetings, there are several parameters to consider: the style, the teeth, the grip.

The Style: Push or Pull
Handsaws cut either on the push stroke (e.g., your dad's old hell-beast, three-foot-long blade coated with rust) or the pull stroke (e.g., the Japanese-style saws now enjoying huge popularity). Trying to cut wood with a push stroke is the equivalent of a Viking flogging, for the following reasons:

1. The saw blade binds, flexes, pinches, warps, and twists, especially if the wood is green and/or wet.

2. Push-saw manufacturers stiffen the blade by making it thicker. This causes the blade to leave a wide, unsophisticated "kerf" (the groove left in the wood by the saw blade).

3. A push saw (especially that rusty old one of your dad's, which is the saw most of us start with) may finish your DIY career the same day it begins.

A proud moment with my Japanese saws.

The Teeth

Large, coarse teeth are best used in "ripping," which is the act of cutting along the grain. For crosscutting (cutting across the grain), a fine-toothed saw cuts a narrow, precise kerf. The higher the number of teeth per inch, the smoother (and slower) the cut.

The Grip

Push saws have large, awkwardly shaped wooden handles that are uncomfortable to use if you have smaller hands. Pull saws often have traditional Japanese bamboo or wood handles. These take some getting used to, but they soon become comfortable. Tool manufacturers have recently introduced pull saws that feature pistol-grip handles loosely based on the traditional North American saw handle. This design feels familiar to people who learned on a push model.

If you're getting into woodworking, a Japanese-style back-saw would be a good choice because it has a stabilizing, rigid spine running along the top of the blade, minimizing wobbly cuts. Some pull-saw models conveniently have a double-edged blade: one side for ripping, one for cross-cutting. They're my favorite. If you buy only one saw in your life, make it a pull saw. It'll cost you roughly thirty bucks, but it's guaranteed not to kill your enthusiasm for handy pursuits. And remember the sawing motto: Pull, don't push, and never pinch. The same goes for social greetings.

Swingin' Stylings

How to choose a hammer

Buying your first hammer is like buying your first bra. You're likely to choose something bigger than what you actually need. This makes other people laugh and point, but there is fierce pride in strapping on that pristine-white badge of maidenhood. The same goes for hammers. You wouldn't have wanted a beaten-up hand-me-down for your first bra, so why content yourself with an inherited hammer?

But here's a warning. The guys who made fun of your first bra are now working at the hardware store. When you tell them you need a hammer, and they smile and say, "What for, ma'am?" don't try a smart comeback based on pubescent humiliations. Maintain your composure, because what they actually want to know is whether you need a smaller (five- to twelve-ounce) hammer for household stuff like installing picture hooks, or a larger (fourteen- to twenty-eight-ounce) hammer for heavier framing or building decks.

It can be confounding to select the best hammer from the array of products available. However, there are really just three things to consider when choosing your personal, life-long hammer: the handle, the head, and the mmm-factor.

The Handle

There are four kinds of handles widely available: steel, fiberglass, graphite, and wood.

A steel shaft is great for really heavy use. It never breaks, but it's the least comfortable to use because the vibration caused by repeated striking will travel up the handle and into your arm, causing tenderness and even tendonitis.

When you're young, you're always getting new things, like teeth, or underarm hair, or hips. It makes you excited and expectant every day. Then when puberty ends and all that stops, you get complacent. But if you learn new skills, unexpected things start happening again. This gives you back your youth, but without the startling body hair.

TIPS

• For maximum comfort, the overall length of your hammer should not be greater than the distance between your fist and your elbow.

• If you want a really small, delicate grip, buy an antique hammer. They usually cost less than $10.

• If you have small hands, Asian hammers often have smaller grips than traditional North American hammers.

A pair to remember.

Fiberglass is somewhat better than steel for vibration. It has great durability, but it is used mostly in heavier models meant for framing and rough construction.

Graphite is being used in a few of the newer hammers. As in high-end tennis racquets and golf clubs, graphite reduces weight and contributes antishock properties. A graphite handle provides up to eight times better vibration reduction compared to an all-steel hammer, and they look so hot, you might not even mind their higher price.

The traditional favorite is the wood-handled hammer. Hickory is the most common wood variety used. The cell structure of this straight-grained wood absorbs much of the vibration, making these hammers pleasant to use.

The Head

Heads are high-carbon steel or, if you're a lucky dog with no budget limitations, titanium. The striking face of the head can be smooth or waffle-textured. If you're into building decks or framing structures, you'll want the textured face because it self-corrects aiming deficiencies by helping the hammer grab the nail head. On the other hand, if you hang pictures using a textured hammer head and miss, you'll leave conspicuous wafflelike scars on all your walls.

The sweet Stanley graphite hammer.

The claw on the other end of the striking head is used for removing nails that went in crooked or bent. (This is never your fault. Some nails just come from the wrong side of the foundry.) Claws come in two styles: curved and straight (known as "rip"). A rip claw has great leverage for removing nails but tends to tear up surfaces, so it's best for rough jobs. A curved claw doesn't readily mark surfaces, so it's better for refined maneuvers.

The Mmm-Factor

The best hammer for your specific grip strength and hand size will make you feel good. You might even feel more competent or slightly smarter. You'll know you've found the right hammer when you hear yourself say, "Mmm."

Some handles are rubber coated to give you a better grip and to reduce vibration. The tactile surface reduces the grip strength required to hold on to the hammer, so your muscles won't get as fatigued. Practice swinging a hammer to feel its balance and personality. Consider the diameter and length of the shaft. If you find that you "choke up" on your grip (by moving your hand closer to the head because the diameter at the bottom of the handle is too stout for your hand), this is not the hammer for you. The right-sized hammer for your hand is one that can be comfortably held near the bottom for maximum swinging force.

It's good to have as many as forty hammers, but you may have to decide which features are most important, and then buy a single hammer accordingly. Pick a hammer that's easy to control but heavy enough to drive the kind of nails you use most often, and soon you'll be banging away with more than your fair share of enthusiasm.

Multitools

The ultimate mood-setter

In the midst of the summer wedding season, you have to wonder how many of the lace-festooned hopefuls in white stretch limos will one day wish they'd never got married. With divorce rates flourishing, the modern bride needs something extra to guarantee that married life will be splendid, fulfilling, and rife with adventure. The modern bride needs a multitool.

In adult life, finding your ideal multitool is similar to discovering love: your pulse quickens, your breathing becomes shallow, your palms dampen, eyes lock without intending to, you don't sleep well. Apply these exact physiological specifications to your selection of a multitool. There are many to choose from but only one will suit you for life, unless you're a multi-multitool girl, in which case, you may also find monogamy challenging. Most multitools have similar features: pliers with both wire-cutting and gripping surfaces, a selection of knife blades, several screwdrivers, a saw blade, ruler, metal file, and that critical mood-enhancing option, the bottle opener.

The bridal garter is incomplete without a multitool.

Why are good tools so tempting? It's because we're primates, and primates gain importance in their tribe when they acquire status, and better tools mean higher status. As you gain status, the level of serotonin (a kind of well-being brain chemical) in your bloodstream rises. More status gives you more serotonin, which is why you crave better tools or a bigger house or a more expensive car. So next time you want something you don't need, just say, "Hey, it's not greed; it's biology." And that makes you either dang clever or the helpless victim of a wanton brain chemical.

A superior multitool has great action. You can whip it out one-handed in a single swift motion. Individual blades pull easily from their nested cradle, and the knives lock for safety. Good multitools also come with a sturdy case that you can strap to your belt, boot, or bra.

Whether you're married or single, a multitool makes a sweet and subtle difference in the quality of your life. Share the joy. Next time you're invited to a wedding, ensure that the bride is given a reasonable start in married life. Give her a multitool. Give the groom one too, if he's the sulky sort. No point clouding the wedding night with tool envy.

Web sites for the multitool enthusiast:

Gerber (www.gerberblades.com) makes a range of multitools. Their unique feature is a cool flip-out pliers head that makes the tool fun to use and great for stirring up dull social functions. Plus you can accessorize them with interchangeable driver bits.

Leatherman (www.leatherman.com) produced the first multitool, so it's been in the game the longest. One of their latest models, which I have yet to be given as a thoughtful surprise for being a nice wife, is the Flair. It encourages an enigmatic lifestyle by providing a corkscrew, butter knife, and cocktail fork in addition to all the usual stuff.

SOG (www.sogknives.com) is my personal favorite at the moment. The action is unbelievably smooth for quick one-handed whip-outs. The hex nuts can be adjusted to make it even faster. This is the only multitool I've found that has a square-head driver bit.

Test Your Screw-Q

A beginner's guide to fasteners

People often ask me about screwing. For example, this recently arrived in my in-box:

I have a problem. I'm trying to put up some plant hangers. I have the stud finder and got everything laid out. I position the screw and can't get it started. I even got the screw lubricant to no avail—just makes it messy, and when I push harder, the screw just jackknifes. What can I do? – Ron Watson

Ron has banged into the First Axiom of Screwing, which states: "The effort to which the screwer goes to ensure an easy, fulfilling screwing experience is inversely proportional to the luck he will have in achieving this goal." Ron's experience was messy and difficult, even with the lubricant. Pushing too hard, too early, is a common technique issue.

Ron can solve his problem by preparing the receiving end, a step many people neglect. If you try to start a screw on a hard surface using a drill, the screw tip will just slide around, missing the mark. If you're using a screwdriver, the screw will jackknife, as in Ron's case.

Predrilling (with a drill bit slightly finer than the shaft of the screw) will ease the screw's entry into the wall. If you don't have an electric drill, use an ice pick or awl to make an indent.

Even more common than botched screwing technique is confusion about which screw to use for any given project. There's more heartbreak in the fasteners aisle than in any other department of the hardware store, except plumbing, which is an endless vortex of hurt.

> The physicist Niels Bohr said, "An expert is a person who has made all the mistakes that can be made in a very narrow field." So to become an expert do-it-yourselfer, simply collect your mistakes and then trade 'em with other handypersons until you've got the whole set.

The ultimate low point is returning screws to the hardware store when you realize they're the wrong size, type, or drive style. This is why the average homeowner has hundreds of little packages of screws in the basement. If all the unused screws in all our basements were placed in a single heap, it would change the angular momentum of the earth.

You can check your Screw-Q with the following quiz, or test a prospective mate to see if he or she is compatible in the basement:

Section 1: Driving Systems

The impression stamped on a screw's head corresponds with the screwdriver you're supposed to use.

Common driving systems.

What is a slot-head?

a. A screw with a single slash on the surface of the head.

b. The earliest driving system and notably the most annoying.

c. A screw that can be tightened or removed in a pinch using a dime or, if you're my brother, an ax.

d. Someone who's slightly smarter than a bonehead.

e. All the above.

What is a Phillips head?

a. A screw with an $\times$ stamped in the head.

b. Easy to remember if you think of crossing the two *l*'s in "Phillips" to make an ×-shape.

c. The most popular screw in America, invented in the 1930s.

d. Way easier to use than a slot-head, unless you're a bonehead.

e. All the above.

What is a Robertson?

a. A screw with a small square recess in the head.

b. Invented in Canada in 1908 by an English entrepreneur.

c. Slow to catch on in America, where it is not called a Robertson but a "square-head."

d. The easiest screw to use, unless you're an American.

e. All the above.

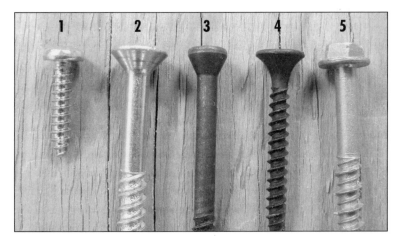

A variety of head profiles.

Section 2: Head Profiles

Identify the screw-head profiles in the above photo.

____ A flat-head wood screw, designed to sit level with the surface, or to be countersunk and covered with wood filler.

____ A heavy-duty hex-head masonry screw for attaching framing to concrete foundations.

____ A pan-head screw, designed to sit proudly on the surface, usually used for assembling metal parts.

____ A trim screw, which trumps a finish nail with its subtle head size and superior gripping power.

____ A drywall screw, designed with soft lines to sit slightly deeper than the drywall surface without puncturing the paper sheathing.

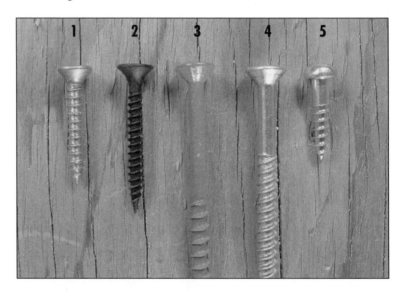

Different types of metal composition.

Section 3: Metal Composition

Screws are made with different materials and/or coatings, depending on intended use. Identify the following screws displayed in the above photo.

____ A wood screw with a ceramic or nylon coating for outdoor use, available in colors that match common wood stains.

____ A drywall screw that rusts like mad outdoors.

____ A shiny electroplated, weather-resistant zinc screw.

____ A solid brass pan-head, which won't corrode but is soft enough to strip if you use a power drill, so a screwdriver is preferable.

____ A small, brass-plated steel wood screw, which is durable, looks good, won't corrode, and *can* be used with a drill.

Section 4: Length and Thickness

Choosing the correct size of screw for any given job is based on

a. Whatever you have in the basement.

b. Whether it's longer and thicker than the one that fell out of the item you're repairing.

c. Whether its length is at least three times the thickness of the material penetrated, unless it's a door and you're hanging a Christmas decoration.

d. A loose combination of a through c, but mostly c.

Section 5: Bonus Trivia

Which historical figure(s) allegedly invented the first screw?

a. Archimedes

b. The Pythagorean philosopher Archytas

c. Adam and Eve

Scoring Key: Correct answers are worth one million points

Section 1: All answers are e

Section 2: 2, 5, 1, 3, 4

Section 3: 3, 2, 4, 5, 1

Section 4: d

Section 5: b — the first screw was invented by Archytas in 5 BC, two centuries before Archimedes and his water screw.

If you scored less than 50 percent, get to your nearest hardware store and work on your screw know-how. It's worth the drive. Get it? Drive! I kill me!

Acknowledgments

I have good friends, better than I deserve considering most of them have been around since the stage when I was far too loud, far too often. I want to thank them here, in print, so everyone else knows how generous they've been. First, the people who keep telling me it's okay to be myself even when it's embarrassing for all of us:
- Cynthia Black and Richard Cohn, Sarabeth Blakey, Jade Chan, Marvin Moore, Carol Sibley, Bill Brunson and Susan Utne at Beyond Words.
- Bridget O'Brien for believing that love is everything.
- Robert Mackwood at Contemporary Management for his vision and steadfast nature.
- Munroe Magruder at New World Library, who said, "Do a book."
- Rick Orchard at the *Toronto Star*, who said, "Do a book."
- Linda Barnard at the *Toronto Star*, who said, "Do a book."
- Len Fortune at the *Toronto Sun*, who said, "Do a book. Include saucy pictures."

And my long-time friends, who probably have a pool going to see who can hang in the longest:
- Shirley Luthman, who never gives up on me.
- Jill Vandal, who also never gives up on me.
- Steve Smith, who should have given up on me long ago but continues to let me believe he won't.
- Daniel Hunter, my irreplaceable husband, who can't give up on me because we have a license that says he isn't allowed to, and I pretty much hold him to that.
- Andrea Mathieson, who greets even my weirdest ideas with an open heart.
- Leah Cherniak, whose sprite and focus I continue to admire.
- Liz Foers, who is eternally helpful.
- Cynthia Dale, who is unfailingly enthusiastic during my awkward bouts of creativity.
- Gillian and Bill Danner, who never cease to be interested and interesting.
- My brother Ted, who once fixed his bicycle with an axe and ended up in the emergency ward — what a role model.
- My brother Alan, who is accurate when he says I should have finished my Physical Education degree by now.

• Rick Green, who believes that nothing is impossible, so we all have to support his little fantasy, and Ava, who loves Rick and also believes that nothing is impossible; what an unbearable couple.
• Kevin and Adrian Campbell, who have huge souls but never complain about the burden until after a few beers.

Since this book won't be eligible for any awards, let this be the speech that won't be heard at any boring ceremonies:

They say that if you take a deep breath, you inhale at least one molecule of Caesar's dying breath. So think how many molecules are available of all your friends' *living* breaths.

If you need to feel better, just breathe deeply and know that you're inhaling molecules that have travelled through the cells of your dearest friends. That'll brings you comfort. And sometimes a squishy feeling in your shoes, but I'm told that's normal. Thank you.

— Your friend,
Mag

OTHER BOOKS FROM
BEYOND WORDS PUBLISHING, INC.

Ripe
The Truth About Growing Older and the Beauty of Getting On with Your Life
Authors: Janet Champ and Charlotte Moore
$19.95, softcover

Ripe: The Truth About Growing Older and the Beauty of Getting on with Your Life is a positive, witty, fearless verbal and visual journey through the confusion, fear, wonder, myths, fictions and facts of facing — and embracing — the inevitable change all women will someday face. It unflinchingly delves into a subject that is still largely taboo and confronts head-on the fact that women "of a certain age" feel discarded and undervalued merely because they have entered the next normal stages of life — peri-menopause, menopause, and all that lie beyond. Unlike many books in this category, *Ripe: The Truth About Growing Older and the Beauty of Getting on with Your Life* is not a compendium of clinical information. From the first page to the last, the authors talk with other women, like themselves, with warmth and wit. Because quite seriously, at times such as these women not only need to laugh, but deserve to. Illustration, photography, and found material are woven throughout to reveal the myriad ways of looking at, dealing with, and understanding society's feelings — and more importantly, our own — about aging, maturing, ripening. These images enrich the conversation, deepen the wit, and drive home the point that this phase of life is redolent of an underappreciated beauty that is much more than skin deep.

The Secret Life of Water
Author: Masaru Emoto
$16.95, softcover

The third book by the author of the best-selling *The Hidden Messages in Water, The Secret Life of Water* concentrates on the power of prayer. Masaru Emoto's hope is to bring the world closer to peace through the use of water. In addition to covering the three aspects of hado — vibration, resonance, and similarity — the most important aspect of hado is the "flow," or circulation. Emoto focuses in depth on this aspect and the consequences of human nature — desire, pride, and ideology — getting in the way of this "flow." *The Secret Life of Water* talks extensively about water's ability to show us the answers — how to live happily, the meaning of loving nature, and the direction we should take. Water can act as a mirror, and the quality of water is a reflection of our hearts. Emoto stresses that the current water situation is serious. The first step toward protecting the earth and water is to focus on our prayers.

Emoto documents the power of prayer when people gather together, and he discusses several experiments which show this. For example, in June 1999, 350 people gathered at Lake Biwa in Japan and prayed for world peace. The water in the lake improved. Similar experiments also resulted in the formation of beautiful water crystals. Water shows us visually that our prayers can change the world. Those who become aware of their role to pray for the betterment of the earth must take action so that others will also follow. In order to facilitate this, Emoto started a project of prayer that occurs on the 25th of each month around the world.

The True Power of Water
Author: Masaru Emoto
$16.95, softcover

Following the release of Masaru Emoto's best-selling book *The Hidden Messages in Water*, *The True Power of Water* takes an in-depth look at how water can be used to improve our health and everyday lives. After Emoto's discovery that molecules of water are affected by thoughts, words, and feelings, his extensive research has yielded groundbreaking discoveries. Emoto discusses how water has the capability to transcribe the information of illness and how people's names and pictures even carry the information of their illness. Emoto also explains the limitations of Western medicine and how many conditions that are thought of as hereditary may not necessarily be so. He also outlines the power of words on illness and how certain words can enhance our immunity.

In *The True Power of Water*, Emoto explains the realizations he gained by combining the results of his latest scientific research with the knowledge he drew from his years of water research projects. Emoto's main objective and passion is the healing of water, mankind, and the earth. He takes this research one step further by providing practical everyday uses for the healing power of water.

The Hidden Messages in Water
Author: Masaru Emoto
$16.95, softcover

New York Times best-selling author Masaru Emoto shares the realizations he has gained by combining the latest scientific research with the knowledge he has drawn from his years of studying water in *The Hidden Messages in Water*. Emoto's main objective and passion is the healing of water, mankind, and the earth. By expressing love to water, one can create a small, beautiful universe. Our consciousness, eyes, and mind, when full of good will, breathe new life into water and help us heal by using the most simple resource, water. His research has visually captured the structure of water at the moment of freezing, and through high-speed photography, Emoto has shown the direct consequences of destructive thoughts or, alternately, the thoughts of love and appreciation on the formation of water crystals. Filled with 64 pages of full-color photographs, and over 100 photographs in total, *The Hidden Messages in Water* provides empowering proof that water is alive and responsive to our every emotion.

The Healing Power of Hado

Authors: Toyoko Matsuzaki, with Natsumi Blackwell

$14.95, softcover

According to ancient Chinese medicine and philosophy, everything releases energy, or chi. In the Japanese spiritual community, hado is a similar life-force energy that encompasses healing properties and transformative powers. Literally translated, it means *wave motion* or *vibration*. Once we become aware of it in our everyday lives, hado can spark great changes in our physical space and emotional well-being. In *The Healing Power of Hado*, Toyoko Matsuzaki shares stories of her experiences as a hado master, demystifies hado energy, and explains how we can access this unique source of power. By tapping into their hado power, beginners can sense the hado of other people, objects, and environments. Advanced practitioners can change physical aspects of their lives (for example, make jewelry sparkle and change the taste of water). Those who practice hado at the master level can heal physical ailments of their own and others, discover their latent clairvoyant abilities, and even receive messages from departed loved ones.

The Gifts of Change

Author: Nancy Christie

$14.95, softcover

The Gifts of Change explores the commonplace activities that are part and parcel of everyday life — an unwelcome gift, an unwanted rejection, an unexpected schedule disruption. Readers are invited to look beyond the surface of occurrence for hidden meanings and subtle truths. The result is a shift in their perceptions about themselves and the life they are living — and the choices they have.

When we welcome change, we find opportunities for growth and development. New strengths and hidden abilities become apparent to us. Life itself becomes an expansive and ever-expanding process. By embracing those changes that come into our lives, we are able to learn from them, ultimately creating a richer, deeper, more fulfilling life.

Live in the Moment

Author: Julie Clark Robinson

$13.95, softcover

Fresh, funny, and blatantly honest, *Live in the Moment* holds the secret to harnessing the power of the present. A practical book about creating one's own life experiences, author Julie Clark Robinson's words of inspiration will help you to create your own mental treasure chest. *Live in the Moment* is for those times when we simply need to stop allowing life's ups and downs to dictate how we feel and look to ourselves to set the tone. If you're willing to lighten up one minute, dig deep the next, and be painstakingly honest throughout, you will come away with a revitalized outlook on life.

Unclutter Your Life
Transforming Your Physical, Mental, and Emotional Space
Author: Katherine Gibson
$14.95, softcover

In this "run-and-grab" world, we stumble over the clutter that invades our homes and workplaces and assaults our minds and emotions. Clutter has us in a vice, and there's no letting go. Katherine Gibson exposes these obstacles for the self-stifling hindrances they are, including the guilt, self-doubt, envy, and toxic relationships that clutter the spirit. She offers tools to understand the physical and psychological chaos and confusion created by clutter and to create your own personal conclusions for restoring peace, harmony, and creativity in your life.

The Truth about Beauty
Transforming Your Looks and Your Life from the Inside Out
Author: Kat James
$17.95, softcover

Nationally renowned holistic beauty expert and celebrity makeup artist Kat James presents a comprehensive health and beauty book that tells readers how to shed toxic and unnatural mind-sets and habits to let their real beauty shine through. Drawing from breaking science and her own remarkable metamorphosis, James offers lifestyle upgrades that can yield stunning physical rewards without drugs, surgery, sweat, or deprivation.

Beyond Stitch and Bitch
Reflections on Knitting and Life
Author: Afi-Odelia Scruggs
$12.95, softcover

For those who knit, this book will remind you why you love this handicraft. Knitting is not only a craft but a hobby, a source of joy, a way to give, and a place to find peace. *Beyond Stitch and Bitch* is a collection of essays that explores the emotional and spiritual experiences common to those who knit. Its engaging, appealing stories chronicle how knitting can be a spiritual, meditative experience and how one can learn patience, creativity, discipline, and diligence from knitting. Intertwined with the essays are knitting patterns with easy how-to steps and photographs.

The Power of Appreciation

The Key to a Vibrant Life

Authors: Noelle C. Nelson, Ph.D., and Jeannine Lemare Calaba, Psy.D.

$14.95, softcover

Research confirms that when people feel appreciation, good things happen to their minds, hearts, and bodies. But appreciation is much more than a feel-good mantra. It is an actual force, an energy that can be harnessed and used to transform our daily life — relationships, work, health and aging, finances, crises, and more. *The Power of Appreciation* will open your eyes to the fabulous rewards of conscious, proactive appreciation. Based on a five-step approach to developing an appreciative mindset, this handbook for living healthier and happier also includes tips for overcoming resistance and roadblocks, research supporting the positive effects of appreciation, and guidelines for creating an Appreciators Group.

This Day

Editors: Joni B. Cole, Rebecca Joffrey, and B. K. Rakhra

$15.95, softcover

Drawn from an extraordinary project in which over 500 women from all walks of life kept "day diaries" on a single day, the collective voices in *This Day* reach across experiential, cultural, geographical, and socioeconomic boundaries. While the deliciously intimate details satisfy even the most shameless curiosity, most importantly, *This Day* reveals the extraordinary in the ordinary — those moments that occur throughout any given day and illuminate who we really are as individuals, as women, and as Americans.

To order or to request a catalog, contact

Beyond Words Publishing, Inc.

20827 N.W. Cornell Road, Suite 500

Hillsboro, OR 97124-9808

503-531-8700

You can also visit our website at *www.beyondword.com*
or e-mail us at *info@beyondword.com*.

Beyond Words Publishing, Inc.

OUR CORPORATE MISSION

Inspire to Integrity

OUR DECLARED VALUES

We give to all of life as life has given us.

We honor all relationships.

Trust and stewardship are integral to fulfilling dreams.

Collaboration is essential to create miracles.

Creativity and aesthetics nourish the soul.

Unlimited thinking is fundamental.

Living your passion is vital.

Joy and humor open our hearts to growth.

It is important to remind ourselves of love.